Clouds
&
Rainbows

Ursula Madden

EDWARD GASKELL*publishers*
Devon

©   Ursula Madden   1996

First Published April 1996
in Great Britain by
EDWARD GASKELL*publishers*
6 Grenville Street
Bideford
Devon
EX39 2EA

Clouds
&
Rainbows

British Library Cataloguing-in-Publication Data
A catalogue record for this book is
available from the British Library

ISBN 1- 898546- 16- 9

Typeset Printed & Bound by
The Lazarus Press
Bideford
Devon EX39 2EA

Acknowledgements

I would like to especially thank the following group of professionals who were interested in the idea of *Clouds & Rainbows* and helped me to keep it going not only during the good periods but also during the frequent and inevitable darknesses, when my spirit flagged and I wanted to give up.

Dr IR Williams	(Consultant Neurologist)
Mrs Mary Baker MBE	(National & International Development Consultant PDS)
Dr JE Anderson	(GP)
Rev M Hickey	(Parish Priest County Durham)
Mr P Rogan	(Formerly Head-Teacher St Michael's School Kirkby)
Mrs B Frost	
Mrs M Grant	} Very Special Friends

Contents

Contents

Dedicated
to
Peter
Nancy Jenny
Rachel & Gregory
who are
'The Wind Beneath My Wings'

Foreword

Parkinson's disease is an illness that affects the learned voluntary actions such as washing, dressing, eating, speaking, driving, playing a musical instrument, making love. This is an illness that affects every part of your life. It is one of the most challenging neurological illnesses and it is so easy to be overwhelmed by the diagnosis and symptoms.

During the years I have worked with the Parkinson's Disease society of the United Kingdom, one of my lasting impressions is to see the varied and courageous ways in which people accept the diagnosis and continue to live their lives. One of the finest examples is Ursula Madden.

I first met Ursula some 5 years ago and have never ceased to be amazed as to where this slim, delicate person finds her energy and determination to live her life to the utmost despite having Parkinson's. She is a mother and grandmother and despite fulfilling all these roles, still has the energy and ability to give beyond her family and friends.

Throughout the years, I have witnessed the chapters of this book emerge and I am truly delighted that at long last Ursula has fulfilled her dream and will receive the recognition she so well deserves. Ursula is a very talented writer and this book will inspire others who have the illness. It will demonstrate very clearly that there is life after Parkinson's disease.

Mary G Baker, MBE
National and International
Development Consultant.

✽

RAINBOWS

Delicate hues in pastel shades,
Nuances of varied light,
I never knew of rainbows
Until there was You.

You walked my way
With gentle step
And blended them
Before my eyes,
I watched in fascination
At the skill
With which you worked.

Your eyes said
I could do it too,
My mind was filled with doubt,
I tried and was amazed to find
That I was wrong
And you were right.

I had the means within me,
Though hidden as it was,
I did not see it shining through
Until there was You.

✽

Chapter 1

THE GOOD LIFE

Thirteen years ago, we were just an ordinary, average, married couple, thirtysomething, both teachers, living in a picturesque little village in the north-west of England. We already had three lovely daughters, Nancy (13), Jenny (11) and Rachel (8). We had recently acquired a son, who, once we had got used to the idea, having hitherto considered our family complete, was welcomed with great joy and affection into our midst. While each of the girls arrived conveniently and with reasonable decorum, more or less on her expected date, he entered our lives with an unexpected flourish, though, to be honest, it was hardly his fault.

On the morning of Friday, September 29th 1978, I awoke at 2 am with severe abdominal pains. The pregnancy still had a good four weeks to go, and although I could not identify these particular pains, having never experienced anything like them before, they in no way resembled labour pains. They were in the region of the lower abdomen and were sharp and constant, unlike labour pains which come and go in waves, gaining strength and frequency gradually.

After three-quarters of an hour, as my condition had not changed, I thought it best to get professional help, and therefore, I phoned the Doctor on call. I explained the symptoms to him, and he replied that he thought they probably denoted a kidney infection, fairly common in late pregnancy. He did not deem it necessary to come out to see me (even though he only lived round the corner), and said he would see me at 9.00 am in the surgery.

Having no other option, I spent the next six hours trying, in vain, to find a suitable position, either standing, sitting or lying, which would give me some relief from the continuous and unrelenting onslaught of pain and discomfort that engulfed me.

On the stroke of 9.00 am, I duly presented myself at the surgery. After a cursory examination, the Doctor told me to go home and wait for an ambulance, which he would summon to take me to the hospital, where they would probably keep me in for observation over the weekend. The ambulance arrived about half an hour later. The two older girls had already gone off to their Secondary school, but six-year-old Rachel was asked, by one of the ambulance men, if she would like to travel in the ambulance with her Mummy. She politely declined the offer, deciding she would rather go in the car with Daddy. (Oh, how I envied her!). Peter and I, after a hurried discussion, decided that he would drop her at his sister, Mary's, and then come on to the hospital.

When I arrived at the hospital, I was whisked immediately to an empty labour ward, where I remained for the rest of the day. A nurse came in and asked me some preliminary questions about the nature of the pain, eg when it had started, how severe it was and if it had altered in any way. The most important thing, as far as I was concerned, was to establish that I was not experiencing labour pains, but that turned out to be the very thing she didn't want to know! She had already decided in her own mind that I was in labour, and nothing I could say to the contrary was strong enough to shake her conviction. So, muttering, what she obviously presumed to be one or two soothing platitudes she hurried out of the room, promising to be back soon. Peter had been advised to go into work and that he would be notified immediately when there was anything to report.

I was left alone for most of the day, except for two very young nurses, who took it in turns, at intervals, to pop their heads round the door and give me a reassuring smile, as much as to say, 'Don't worry! We know best!' At one point, I had one visitor – a resident from the psychiatric ward, who bravely attempted to hold a conversation with me, but when he realised that for some unknown reason, I was only able to speak in monosyllables, he gave me a blank stare and shuffled out again no doubt saying to himself: '...And they think I'm mad! – She should be certified!'

By the time four o'clock came, I had had enough! I was still in considerable discomfort and anxious for something to be done towards discovering the cause and dealing with it. Therefore, the next time one of the student nurses looked in, I demanded to see someone in authority. She was about to make some excuse, but one look at my face must have warned her that I was in no mood to brook any further opposition (I don't often get out of my pram, but when I do.... *Look Out*!). She scuttled out of the room and reappeared a couple of minutes later, with Sister-in-Charge following closely on her heels. She advanced towards me, wearing the classic 'I'm not having any nonsense from you – you'll do as you're told' look on her face. This would normally have been enough to intimidate me because, generally speaking, I tend to avoid confrontations wherever possible, but this time things had gone too far and therefore, throwing caution to the winds, I matched her steely glare and repeated with icy emphasis the one fact that I had to get into someone's head: – '*I am not in Labour*!' She responded by raising her eyebrows, shaking her head and announcing that she would prove me wrong by using a monitor. She proceeded to do this, and was astonished to discover that she was the one to be proved wrong, even though she had never experienced labour pains herself. I assured her that, once experienced, they were not easily forgotten even after a gap of six years!

Anyway, to give her her due, now that she had been convinced, she began to take action immediately. She hurried out of the room to find a doctor and came back about five minutes later with a dark, anxious-looking youngish man of eastern origin, wearing a white coat and a nervous smile. I gave as cheerful a smile as I could muster, hoping to put him more at ease, but the minute he opened his mouth, I realised the reason for his nervousness and my heart sank to my feet while my smile froze on my face. He spoke little or no English, and relied heavily for communication on a primitive form of sign language that he was obviously making up on the spur of the moment! 'Oh my God,' I thought, 'I'll be lucky if I come through this alive!'

He set about examining me, and I tried to lie as still as I could while he pushed, prodded, pressed and poked around my substantial tummy, pausing every now and then to enquire if it hurt. After a few minutes, he looked up with a bewildered expression on his face and without speaking, walked over to the window where he and Sister had a brief consultation, consisting mainly of a few weird signs punctuated by the odd word from him and a series of vigorous nods from her. When they returned, Sister asked me if I had ever had a problem with my appendix. I remembered that years ago, while still at school, I had had what was always referred to as a 'grumbling appendix'. When this message was conveyed to the doctor, his face broke into a smile and his sigh of relief was audible in the hushed atmosphere. His decision had been made for him. He now knew what he would do. He left Sister to explain while he busied himself making preliminary arrangements. Sister announced that he had decided to remove my appendix, which was normally a relatively simple operation. What would make this particular case a little more complicated was the fact that the baby was due to be born in a month's time. She said the doctor who had just examined me, had gone to phone the obstetrician to decide how to proceed. She then left me for about fifteen minutes.

When she reappeared, I noticed her face was a little flushed and she could hardly contain her excitement as she explained that the obstetrician had made the decision to perform a caesarean operation first and this would leave the way clear for the other surgeon to perform the appendectomy. Then, saving the best to the last, she leaned a little closer to me and informed me in conspiratorial tones: – 'This is the first time that this has happened in this hospital'. If this piece of news was intended to cheer me, it fell far short of the mark! On the contrary, it terrified me half out of my wits, and my body, rigid with fear, seemed to turn to stone. Fortunately, Peter reappeared a couple of minutes later, having been informed of the situation on his way in. As is his wont in times like this, he was a tower of strength and comfort to me, and after we had been left alone to discuss it thoroughly, I became considerably calmer and realised that there was nothing for it but to trust in God, and cope as best I could for the sake of Peter, the three girls and, of course, this new baby who, through no fault of his own, was now playing a major part in the drama. Having been informed that Nancy and Jenny were being looked after by some very good friends of ours who lived in the village, I was quite amused to hear that they had been taken to see a film called 'Freaky Friday'. The title seemed to fit the bill perfectly!

At 6.00 pm, the obstetrician came on duty, and things started to move at last. While I was prepared for surgery, Peter was ushered into the waiting room, where he was told he would be kept informed of every development. The nurse told him that the caesarean operation would take about half-an-hour and that she would come straight afterwards to let him know about the baby. In actual fact, Peter mentioned later, it turned out to be a lot longer before he heard anything, and he was becoming anxious and was particularly glad to have the company of George, his brother-in-law, who kindly stayed with him through to the end.

As I was recovering from the effects of the double operation, I remember a nurse leaning over me and saying: 'Mrs Madden – *You've got a little boy*'. No one was more surprised than I.

I had been unable to see him for a couple of days, except through the nursery window – because I was not very well and he was a little jaundiced – and the minute I held him in my arms for the first time, I fell in love with him as I had with each of the girls, and looked forward to getting to know him.

A little Chinese nurse said to me the next day: 'Mrs Madden, you must give this baby a name. We can't keep calling him Baby Madden!' We had chosen the name Sophie for a girl, but we had not found one for a boy on which we could agree. Peter, for some unknown reason, wanted the name Bede! I flatly refused, on the grounds that the poor child would be nick-named 'Rosary' at school and would be teased unmercifully. We decided to let the girls' choose between Simon and Gregory. Simon was an unpopular choice because they believed he might be called 'Simple' at school. So Gregory was finally chosen and approved of unanimously. After a fortnight we were both allowed to go home, where we soon settled back into a normal happy routine, unaware that in another three years' time Peter and I would be visiting another hospital for a very different reason. One that would turn our cosy little world upside-down and life would never be the same again.

BIRTH DAY

As sure as night
Must follow day
So joy shall follow
Sorrow.

A mother's pain when giving birth,
Her tension and her anguish,
Is all forgot when at the end,
She holds her baby in her arms.

The silkiness of new-born skin,
The softness of the downy hair,
The cradled head against her breast,
The tiny fingers clench'd.

Each one of these brings untold bliss
With each successive birth,
She feels almost her heart will burst,
So boundless is her love.

What greater happiness exists
In human understanding?
What better proof of Loving God
Who gives such gifts as these.

✿

CONSOLATION

Along the rough and stony road,
With failing heart and faltering step,
My lonely trek began.
The sun had left the darkened sky,
Potential dangers lurked
. In gathering gloom.
Despair's cold fingers clutched
Around my heart and
In the desolate waste
Surrounding me
My eyes could find no exit,
No way out.
Panic surged within me
Turning fast to empty numbness.

And then it was
With gentle touch,
You made your presence known,
You reached deep down within me
And released my anchor'd spirit.

Filled with new life
By the warmth of your love,
It soared above my troubled mind
And came to rest on Hope
As a butterfly on sunshine.

And thus, for now,
It shall remain,
Swaying on emotional breeze,
In fluttering anticipation
Of eventual solution.

Chapter 2

GATHERING CLOUDS

I had suspected that I might have PD (Parkinson's Disease) for two or three years before the actual diagnosis, and I asked my GP, whose opinion I respected, to refer me to a Specialist. He did not share my anxieties about my symptoms, considering them to be due merely to a lack of co-ordination rather than to a specific medical condition, and was therefore very reluctant to comply with my request. I knew nothing about the disease at that time, apart from the fact that one of the symptoms is a distinct tremor, which I had certainly noticed in my right hand, together with a certain rigidity and slowness of movement. As I had always been of a nervous disposition, even as a child, these things did not occur dramatically, all of a sudden, but took on a much more gradual significance, at first noticeable only to myself. However, as time went on, I became increasingly concerned and anxious to get an informed diagnosis which would either dispel my fears once and for all, or confirm them and, hopefully, suggest some kind of treatment. Therefore, when a new GP joined the Practice, I made an appointment to see her, explained the problem and asked to be referred to a Specialist, which she readily agreed to arrange for me.

In due course, I received an appointment card to see a Consultant Neurologist at Wigan Hospital. When I arrived, accompanied by my husband, the Waiting Room to which we were directed, on that first occasion,

9

and indeed, on all subsequent visits, filled me with anxious foreboding. It was not really a room, but a corridor, dark and narrow, containing only one small, opaque window, high up on the wall at one end. A serried row of seats ran the length of the corridor on either side, and the whole area was filled to capacity with patients, of every shape and size, displaying symptoms of what seemed to me to be just about every neurological problem known to man and a few more besides! There was a series of doors on one side, and by keeping my eyes glued (by way of a diversion) to each of these in turn I soon deduced, being of average intelligence, that the one at the top of the corridor, nearest to the window was the 'Holy of Holies', ie the consulting room, and the remainder were examination cubicles, washroom, etc.

As I sat surveying the scene, and patiently awaiting my turn to be ushered behind the hallowed doors, I became aware of an atmosphere of tension and heaviness in the air, which, naturally, did nothing to allay my own private fears. Eventually, after a wait of about an hour and a half, which made nonsense of the time stated on the appointment card, my name was announced and I was duly escorted into the presence of the Almighty (the Consultant), an unremarkable-looking middle-aged man, who sat behind his desk, flanked by two young people in white coats, who appeared uncomfortable and ill at ease. Dispensing with what he obviously considered to be unnecessary pleasantries, the Consultant, after a curt nod, glanced down at the notes on the desk in front of him and immediately asked a few perfunctory questions – the answers to which he seemed to find singularly uninteresting. He then barked out an order and without further ado, the Commanding Officer (Sister), who had evidently been waiting in the wings in order to appear on cue, took hold of my arm in a vice-like grip and frog-marched me to an examination cubicle, where I was subsequently given instructions to undress to my underwear, lie on the couch, and cover myself with the sheet provided. I was then, mercifully, left alone for ten to fifteen minutes, during which time I tried in vain to recover my composure and stop my limbs from shaking. At the end of this interval, the curtain was swept aside with a flourish and in strode the Sergeant-Major of the piece (the Consultant). Without saying a word, or even glancing at me, he began at once to pick up each of my limbs in turn, hold them suspended for a moment, and then drop them again (I have since come to the conclusion that he was probably testing for rigidity, but at the time, I was not enlightened and had no idea as to the significance of the exercise). When he had finished, he looked at me solemnly and pronounced the words *It is Parkinson's* in an ominous voice. Whereupon, he turned upon his heel and made a swift exit, leaving the words ringing in my ears.

After a few minutes, during which time I made a further effort to calm my frayed nerves – reminding myself that it was, after all, only a confirmation of what I had more or less expected – the nurse put her head round the curtain and told me to get dressed again and return to the waiting-room. Having done this, which took longer than I expected because I was thoroughly unnerved, I barely had time to whisper a few hurried words to Peter about what had occurred, before I was recalled into the Presence. This time Peter was allowed, albeit somewhat grudgingly, to join me.

As we walked in, He was engaged in giving a hurried explanation to the two nervous students, who, although listening intently, so as not to have to ask for a repetition, were still looking as anxious and unhappy as before. They gave the impression that this encounter with their CO was every bit as much of an ordeal for them as it was for me! I found myself feeling compassionate and 'motherly' towards them. However, a moment later I forgot them and once more quailed at the stern, harsh voice which I realised was, this time, directed at me. With a conscious effort I forced myself to face the hard, glaring eyes, in which I was unable to detect the slightest compassion or sympathy with regard to the severity of the sentence he had passed on me only a few minutes before. He informed me in clipped, curt tones, that I would be required to spend a week in hospital in order to have certain tests carried out, which would ultimately confirm the diagnosis. In his mind, there was no doubt whatsoever. He said he would arrange for the hospital to phone as soon as there was a bed available, and as it was now late November, it would probably be before Christmas. His duty done, and obviously not one to waste any precious time on niceties, he perfunctorily dismissed us and demanded to see the next patient. We were left together – with our shattered nerves, anxious thoughts and unanswered questions, to find our way out of the 'warren' and back to the car-park as best we could.

As we made our way to the car, several large drops of rain managed to penetrate the dense clouds overhead and two or three minutes later, these erupted into a steady downpour which suited our mood perfectly. I was reminded of the old Buddy Holly hit, *Raining in my Heart*. We spoke very little as we drove home, but the empathy between us made words superfluous. Peter reached across and squeezed my hand and I remember thinking at the time how aptly, albeit unwittingly, his parents had named him – Peter, the rock. I had little doubt that he would prove to be my strong and steady rock, supporting and comforting me thoughout the harrowing days that lay ahead.

HOW MUCH

You ask how much I need you,
In truth I answer thus:
As much as plants need water,
And humans, nourishment.

You are for me essential,
A necessity of life,
For gentle warmth to aid my growth,
For sustenance by which I live,
As indispensable as air.

Don't ever leave me, my sweet love,
I need your tenderness
To solace and to comfort me
When God seems not to hear.

❀

THE DARK SIDE OF THE SUN

There is a dark side to the sun,
I've seen it many times,
My shadowy fears still linger there,
In spectral form they lurk,
Waiting for their chance to strike
When I am vulnerable

When all is still and silent
and the birds no longer sing,
The sun begins to weaken,
Its brightest rays to fade,

T'is then these apparitions
Assume their monstrous shapes,
advancing ever nearer
With menacing effect.

I cannot see them clearly,
Yet I know that they are there,
Hovering in the darkness
Somewhere above my head,

Conspiring with the swaying trees
And whispering gently to the breeze,
They lay their snares with confidence
Knowing victory is sure.

Unable to withstand
The fierceness of their onslaught,
I cringe and cower within their grasp,
Twisting first this way, then that,
Seeking vainly to escape
Their suffocating hold.

But even as I struggle,
I know I cannot win,
That feeble flame within me
That burns erratically,

That weak and wayward spirit,
Lacking strength to overcome,
Will let itself be trampled on
And ground into the dust.

Its struggles ineffectual
'Gainst the vigour of the foe,
Inevitably acknowledge
Its subsequent defeat.

And in the final deathly throes
My battered spirit yields,
And creeps away to hide its shame
In friendless solitude.

The victors then proclaim success
And celebrate with joy,
Then slinking back from whence they came
They live to fight another day.

Chapter 3

A WEEK BEHIND BARS

We waited about three weeks before the dreaded summons arrived in the form of a phone call. They should have been happy, busy days, working up to the excitement of preparing for Christmas, a time we usually enjoyed. Instead, they passed slowly, fraught with tension and anxiety. Every little irritation was blown up out of all proportion. The children wandered forlornly about the house, wearing puzzled frowns more often than smiles on their faces. I had been told that I would be required to go into one of the old, established teaching hospitals in Manchester, so I realised that there would be students there. When I answered the phone, I was instructed, in painfully slow, stunted English, to check-in at the hospital at about nine-thirty the following morning. The rest of the day passed in a haze of despondency, during which I performed the necessary domestic tasks in robot-fashion, answering the children's inevitable queries in preoccupied monosyllables. We ate our evening meal in virtual silence, only speaking when necessary. The girls took their cue from us and behaved in similar fashion. Little Gregory, toddler though he was, sensed something was wrong, and played with his beloved cars on the low window-sill with a much-diluted enthusiasm. Even the fresh flowers in their vases seemed to droop in sympathy! The rest of the evening passed without incident and the morning dawned cold and cheerless. We had thought it best to try and keep things as normal as possible for the girls, so they went to school as usual. We had arranged for Gregory to have a little holiday with his grand-parents in Wilmslow. He had been looking forward to it and raised no objection when they came to pick him up. He waved happily from the back window as they turned the corner, and though I was hard-pressed to keep back the tears, it was good to know that he was in safe hands, and that I would have no reason to worry about him.

The hospital was indeed old – so old it was almost obsolete. The outside was dark and drear and I was somewhat dismayed to find that the inside was no more welcoming. When we arrived at the enquiry desk, we were directed to the Neurology unit by a tall, thin receptionist who was obviously afraid to smile in case her face cracked in the process! After we had filled in the appropriate forms, we were escorted, by a student nurse, to the ward. As soon as I set eyes on it, I was appalled at the spectacle, which was, to my mind, something very much akin to pictures I had seen of a nineteenth century lunatic asylum! I would have given anything to be able to say, 'forget it' and go back home, but I felt I needed to know for sure, for the sake of the family, as well as for myself, and it was a necessity that could be delayed no longer.

The ward was a large room, which had, at some stage, been partitioned off, as cheaply as possible, into sections of four – the overall effect was of 'organised chaos'. People with various complaints, of which the majority, though not all, were neurological, were wandering around aimlessly, looking for someone to talk to, or to congregate in the toilet block in order to smoke a cigarette. Some, who were attached to drips, shuffled along trailing their appendages with them. I followed the nurse, with growing uneasiness, to the far end of the ward, where I was allocated a bed between a very old lady, obviously nearing the end of her days, and consequently oblivious of all the activity going on around her, and a young girl of about twenty, whom I warmed to immediately, because hers was the only friendly face I had seen since I had first arrived.

The nurse drew the curtains, and told me to change into night-wear and get into bed, and that a doctor would be along shortly to examine me. Peter was summarily dismissed a few minutes after I got into bed, and about twenty minutes later, a studious-looking young man in a white coat appeared in my cubicle, clutching a stethoscope in one hand, and introduced himself unsmilingly, as Dr Keogh. When he spoke, I identified his voice as the one I had heard on the phone the previous day. Noting the gaucheness of his movements, and the way in which he handled his instruments during the ritual of examination, I deduced that he was more likely to be a student still early on in his training, rather than a fully-fledged doctor. I've often wondered why so many medical students deem it necessary to try to deceive patients in this way, by pretending to be fully qualified when they are not. They seem to think our brains are routinely extracted at the entrance to the hospital! If they would simply admit the truth, and ask for help in a friendly manner, patients would probably be more inclined to be co-operative. I have usually found it a relief to know that they are supervised by their superiors, who, rightly, take the responsibility of making the ultimate decisions. This young man, however, had nothing at all to say to me. He conducted his examination in stony silence, his expression unchanging. When he had finished it, he walked straight out again, without a backward glance. Many times during that week, students would come – sometimes alone and sometimes with a partner – to examine me, presumably because, being still in my thirties and therefore comparatively young to have contracted Parkinson's Disease, I was considered an interesting phenomenon. Often during the proceedings, I was asked to get out of bed, remove my gown and parade up and down the cubicle in front of them, so they could identify certain recognised symptoms. I did not feel that I had grounds for complaint in this instance, because nothing untoward ever happened, but nevertheless, I felt uncomfortable and embarrassed, and in addition, somehow 'used' and even a little degraded.

After my preliminary examination, I drew back the curtains round the bed and introduced myself to the girl in the next bed. Her name was Chris, she was nineteen years old and she lived with her boyfriend. When I asked why she was in hospital, she explained that a few days earlier, on waking up in the morning, she found herself suddenly paralysed from the waist downward. There didn't seem to be any logical reason for this, so she had been referred by her GP to the hospital for tests to try to discover the root cause. She'd had certain tests in the last few days, but there was still no satisfactory explanation. However, she wasn't prepared to let it get her down and I admired her for her resilience and strength of character. She was very lively, and in the gruelling days that followed I was grateful for her cheerfulness and ready wit. Later that day, I suddenly felt very tired and lay back on the pillows with my eyes closed. I didn't sleep but I was dozing comfortably, when something made me open my eyes. The next moment I was wide awake and feeling decidedly anxious. There was a middle-aged woman sitting on my bed, staring at me, with a strange, vacant expression in her eyes. I didn't dare move. I just stayed exactly as I was and stared back at her, wondering what on earth she was going to do next. I heard a low chuckle coming from somewhere nearby and recognised it as Chris's. I glanced briefly at her, and she must have seen the fear in my eyes, for she immediately stopped laughing and said, 'Don't worry, she's not singling you out. She does that to everyone. When she gets tired of your face, she'll get up and wander to someone else's bed and give them the same treatment. She does it all the time.'

I tried to relax a little, but remained as motionless as I could, not wishing to frighten her by any sudden movement. After a while, she got up and wandered off towards another bed, just as Chris had said she would. However, she was back again at least twice a day. When she was there, staring at me, I felt intimidated and never took my eyes off her, just in case she took it into her head to do something unexpected. Chris christened her 'Wandering Winnie', which summed her up nicely.

When I ventured to look out of a window, I realised we were on the top floor, which probably accounted for the iron bars, which gave me a feeling of claustrophobia – hence the title of this chapter. Since the only things to be seen from those windows were rows upon rows of slate roof-tops, a sight which I found singularly depressing, it did not seem to matter.

The following morning, I had to have various tests, including a blood-test and an ECG, conducted with very little social contact, giving me the now familiar sensation of being a 'specimen' rather than a person. When I got back to the ward, I found that Chris had also been transported somewhere, so I settled down to read for a while. I had not expected any visitors, because it was a fairly long trip to Manchester from Parbold and, in any case, Peter had his hands full looking after the girls as well as doing a full time teaching job. So it was a complete surprise when, at about 1.00 pm, a nurse came to inform me that I had a visitor. I thought she must have made a mistake, but when he appeared, I recognised him as the husband of one of the first friends I had made when we first came to live in Parbold. The circumstances being as they were, I was so delighted to see a familiar face from my personal world, that I immediately dropped my book, threw my arms around him and gave him an enthusiastic hug, thereby endangering the fragile lives of the flowers he held in one hand, not to mention the chocolates he held in the other. He obviously had not expected such a welcome, and probably thought he really had come to a mad-house! As it was officially lunch-time and therefore not an authorised visiting time, as the ward-sister was quick to point out, David was only allowed to stay for a few minutes, but I shall always remember that visit, which did more for me at that particular time, than all the medicine in the world could have done!

The following morning, the Consultant miraculously appeared with a dozen or so students in tow. At this point, I should tell you that this worthy gentleman had graduated from a military man to the dizzy heights of the super-natural, which of course, requires a brief explanation. During that particular week, I had caught glimpses of him striding forth purposefully, his gleaming white coat billowing around him, and closely followed by a host of minions also clad in white coats, each one with an anxious expression, hanging on to his every word, no doubt aspiring to emulate him as a high-flyer in the medical sphere. Consequently, I felt it necessary to elevate him to a position more befitting his station. I, therefore privately re-named him, 'Michael the Arch-angel', by which title he remained throughout the rest of our acquaintance. He explained to me, in laymen's terms, the problem that occurs in Parkinson's Disease. He explained that it was caused by a chemical imbalance in the brain. To illustrate this, he drew a rough diagram of two chemical flasks, one full of a substance, the other only half full. He then identified the full one as the normal one and the other as abnormal. In other words, in the case of the second one, the brain is unable to manufacture enough of the substance, Dopamine, to function normally, and it is this puzzling deficiency which brings about the symptoms of Parkinson's Disease.

During the remainder of the week, I had other tests, too numerous to mention, including a brain scan. This involved lying on a trolley, and having my head inserted into something resembling a washing machine. It made a lot of noise and was a little uncomfortable but it wasn't as daunting an experience as I had expected it to be. The next day, which was Thursday, Michael the Arch-angel visited me again and announced that all the tests had been done and as a result, his original diagnosis had proved to be correct, and that he had therefore prescribed some medication for me to start while still in hospital, in case I had a negative reaction. Sister brought the first dose to me just before dinner. I was to take Madopar 250 four times a day at four hourly intervals. I took the first dose and promptly brought it straight back. Sister, who made it plain that she was not tolerating any of this type of insubordination on her ward, gave as good as she got and insisted that I take another dose immediately and this time, keep it down, or else there would be dire consequences!

That afternoon Chris, who seemed to be slowly beginning to improve, told me that her Consultant was now of the opinion that the birth-control pill was the cause of her paralysis, and that it was just a matter of time before she regained the use of her legs. He had also said that she could go home the next day. I was delighted for her, because she had always remained positive throughout her ordeal, and she had planned to get married in two months time. However, I did not relish the thought of coping in there without her. Two days earlier, a patient with *Tourette's Syndrome* was admitted. This is a serious and distressing condition which causes the sufferer to swear compulsively and use abusive language continuously. This unfortunate lady was put in a bed straight opposite me. Her constant and relentless torrent of abuse which, because of her proximity, seemed to be directed at me, unnerved me to such an extent that I could not get into bed and go to sleep. Instead I sat up on a straight-backed chair, alert and poised ready for flight in case she should try to get out of bed. Although Chris did not share my irrational fear, she understood it and I derived comfort from knowing she was near and I could waken her if I felt the need.

Chris's Mum and Dad and her fiancé came to pick her up on Friday morning at about 11.00 am and I accompanied her to the lift. We had exchanged addresses and phone numbers and promised to keep in touch. All that was left to do was to give each other a hug and good luck wishes, which we did enthusiastically. I walked back to the ward feeling already a little lonely.

I had, by this time, stopped having side-effects with Madopar, and I was agreeably surprised at the difference it made. I noticed especially that I could write legibly without having to hold my right hand steady and I could speak loudly enough for people to be able to hear what I said the first time. Michael the Arch-angel popped his head in briefly that afternoon and left permission with Sister-in charge that I could go home the following day. She almost skipped up the ward, so delighted was she at the prospect of getting rid of me! I was no less delighted, I can tell you.

Peter and the girls came to pick me up the next morning, and as we drove away from the hospital, I made a private vow that I would never again go voluntarily into hospital. I had no intention of ever repeating that horrendous experience. My parents arrived with Gregory soon after we got home, and Peter produced a chocolate cake with which to celebrate our reunion.

ENDLESS NIGHT

The night is long and arduous
For deeply troubled minds,
As through its murky tunnels
They trudge their weary way.

In vain they search for answers,
For some resolving clues,
Yet the more intense their efforts
The more enmesh'd do they become,
Entangled in the undergrowth
Of wretched indecision.

O God, if you be merciful
Where is your mercy now?
Your wisdom and compassion
For these weak and helpless souls?

O come, I do beseech you,
Come quickly to our aid,
And bring for consolation
The healing powers of Dawn.

❀

BURIED TREASURE

His gentleness resembles nothing
I have ever known,
It nestles deep within his heart
Reluctant to appear
A rich a precious jewel
Encased in velvet sheen.

But when at last it does emerge
To face the light of day,
Summon'd from its hiding place
By grave and heartfelt anguish,
Why then it starts to prove its worth,
And illustrate its power,
By pouring forth its therapy,
Enveloping the pain,
Enfolding it in warmth and love
And softening the impact.

Compassion all-embracing
Soothes the sorely-troubled mind,
Providing opportunity
For thought and inspiration.

The struggling Spirit can now at last
Begin its upward climb
From out the depths of loneliness,
That dark and friendless waste,
Into the sunlit sphere of Hope
Companionship and joy.

To feel once more
The fresh, clean air,
The freedom from restriction,
That's brought about by empathy
And unfeigned understanding.

Chapter 4

TAKING STOCK
AND MAKING DECISIONS

At first, I was very impressed with the effect of the medication I had been given. It appeared that our friend, Michael the Arch-angel, regardless of his personal manner, certainly knew what he was talking about when it came to PD. He had told me that if I took the medication regularly, I would be able to continue teaching up until retirement. I was agreeably surprised to hear that. I had trained as an Infants Teacher, and I had always enjoyed my work. At this time, I was doing Supply-Teaching in three surrounding areas in both Junior and Infant Departments. Although I was reasonably content with the Junior classes, I have to admit that I really preferred the Infant age-range. The little ones were always very receptive and enthusiastic. They threw themselves happily into every activity and their lively minds made them ask interesting questions such as: 'Miss, where does the writing go when you rub it out?'

Incidentally, we lived for five years in Canada when my two eldest children were small and for a couple of years I taught a Junior Kindergarten class, which was similar to a Nursery class here. The children attended school for half a day, so that there were twenty children in the morning and then twenty different ones in the afternoon. One very cold Winter's day, everyone had gone home except for one little boy, who could not find his over-boots. In the interests of fostering a desire for independence, I used to encourage the children to do as much for themselves as they were able. Consequently, getting dressed in outdoor clothes had to begin, for the morning class, at 11.45 am so that they would all be ready by 12.00 noon, at which time their parents came to collect them. The afternoon class began at 1.15 pm and I had to have lunch and then prepare the classroom again for the afternoon session.

The most awkward item of clothing for the children to manage was their over-boots, because, of course, they had to fit them over their shoes. On this particular day, the children had all gone except for Craig, who was doing a marathon search with an anxious look on his face. I started to help him and within a few minutes I noticed a pair of red over-boots under a bench, along a side wall. I called to him. 'Craig! Here they are!' He bounded over to me immediately, his little face wreathed in smiles. His joy was short-lived, however, for he took one look at them and announced in a forlorn voice: 'No, Miss, they're not mine.'

'Well, let's just try them on anyway', I said, trying to keep the feeling of exasperation out of my voice. 'They're red, they fit you and they are the only ones here.' He shook his head sadly. 'Why are you so sure they are not yours, darling?' I said in a gentle voice. It wasn't like him to be deliberately awkward.

The answer came back clear and confident: 'Mine had snow on, Miss!' I hugged him and then collapsed into a heap. For once, words failed me!

Yes, my teaching career holds many happy memories for me and I can look back on it with joy. It wasn't all plain-sailing though and, as time went on, there were more and more problems to contend with. Looking back, I think perhaps the main stumbling-block at this time was that I simply could not accept the fact that I had a progressive, degenerative condition, for which

there was no cure and which would slowly but relent-
lessly take control of my body, thereby robbing me of
every ounce of the thing I most valued – namely my
hard-earned independence. I was determined that this
would not happen and resolved to fight it every step of
the way. Unfortunately, I greatly underestimated its
strength and in so doing, chose the wrong weapon. I
elected to ignore it, to repudiate its very existence, to
utterly deny its credibility at every opportunity, in the
vain hope that it would disappear, defeated. Needless
to say, it did not. I had a lot to learn!

I returned to work after Christmas, and behaved as
though nothing had happened. I had to take four pills
a day: one after breakfast, one after lunch, one after
tea and another one at bed-time. This meant that I
only had to take one (after lunch) during school time. I
never took it in the Staff-Room, or anywhere were
there were other people, who might have asked awkward questions. I always retired to the Staff
Cloakroom and swallowed it with water from a running tap. If anyone was already in there, I would comb
my hair and chat until they left. If a child noticed my
hand shaking and asked why, I used to say it was
because I was cold.

I continued with my appointments with Michael the
Arch-angel, at first every three months, but I found
them very galling and invariably frustrating, because
there were so many things I wanted to know about it
and each time, he flatly refused to even listen to my
queries, let alone attempt to answer them, with always
the same excuse – that he had too many other people
to see. There were also times when, even though he
was present in his own consulting room, some patients
(myself included) would be directed into a different
room to see an under-graduate, who, although usually
polite, did not have the knowledge or experience to be

able to answer the questions I wanted to ask. All they could do was to recognise the symptoms and tell me that if I had to suffer from a neurological illness, then PD was the best one to have. I'm sure you can imagine how much comfort I derived from statements of that kind!

About four or five years after the diagnosis, I was formally discharged by my Consultant, which came as a shock to me, because I had been given no intimation at all that such was his intention. By way of explanation, he said that my condition seemed to be stable, that there was nothing else he could do for me at this stage and that I should make another appointment only if and when I felt it to be necessary.

Outwardly, I appeared to approve of this decision. I tried to take it as a positive sign, that he believed it was possible for me to cure myself. But deep down inside myself, it was another story. I knew perfectly well that the real reason for my discharge was that he wanted to shorten his lists of NHS patients. I seemed, perhaps, to be coping quite well and, even more important, it would mean an end to all those questions, which he had neither the time nor the inclination to answer. I did not like the idea of being solely responsible for myself in this instance. I felt vulnerable and gravely uneasy, well aware that I needed some informed medical support, even if it were only the basic, insufficient support that I got from him -- anything was better than nothing. Fortunately, the one thing I did have at this time, was a good relationship with my GP. I could talk freely with her and she always took time out to listen, and I was grateful for her continued support. She did not profess to know very much about my condition and I respected her honesty in this regard. She treated me as an equal and not as a person of inferior intelligence, which had hitherto been my experience with medical staff. At this juncture, she explained that she did not know of another Consultant to whom she could refer me, but that she would make enquiries and be on the look-out for one. In the meantime, all we could do was to pool our small reserves of experience, and make what adjustments we thought would be safe and at the same time, effective.

At this stage I was working full time, doing a long-term supply job for someone who had taken maternity leave. It was at a school in Kirkby, on Merseyside, and I had taken over the Reception class. The policy there, was to admit one or two children at a time, which worked quite well. It meant that I could give the ones who were already settled in, something to do, so that I could spend some time with the new little ones. I caused much merriment amongst the members of my own family, when I went home one day and related that one of the new admissions had worked himself up into a near-hysterical state, repeatedly shouting, 'I've lost my bottle!' Not being acquainted with this expression and in an effort to stop the hysteria from escalating, I asked innocently: 'Well, where did you leave it?'

In all, I did three long-term supplies there at St. Michael's and though the work was hard and the children demanding, I thoroughly enjoyed my time there. The children were willing, enthusiastic and affectionate and the Head Teacher and his Staff were always friendly, amenable and ready to help if necessary. In the meantime, although I was reluctant to admit it even to myself, my disability was slowly creeping up on me and interfering with the things I wanted to do. For instance, I began to have difficulty writing on the black-board. I am naturally right-handed and my right-hand side was the one most affected. There was only one thing to do – learn to use my left hand, which I finally mastered with a passable degree of success. I remembered my College tutor constantly reminding me that we must never present the children in our care with anything that was not perfect and I reflected wistfully that if I were to adhere too closely to that precept, the children I taught would be in danger of getting nothing at all!

It was about this time that my voice, which had never had a great deal of volume, began to be a serious problem in that although it sounded loud enough to me, it made no impression whatever on a class of enthusiastic youngsters, each absorbed in his own occupation! It was not easy to think up a solution but I was determined not to be beaten, and have to back down over something so basic as that. Over a weekend I came up with an idea.

I had once been given a little brass bell made in the shape of a lady wearing a long skirt. I took it into school and explained to the children that her name was '*Tinkerbelle*' and she was going to help me in a very special way. When I had something important to say to all of them, she would help me by ringing her bell. Every time they heard her, they were to stop whatever they were doing (including talking), put down whatever they were holding and raise both hands up high in the air. It worked a treat! They loved '*Tinkerbelle*' and always listened to her messages. (Incidentally, I soon learned that it would be necessary to make a rule that I was the only person allowed to touch her, otherwise the result would be utter chaos!)

Meanwhile, life on the domestic front was continuing as near to normal as was possible. It was Nancy's GCSE year and although she had always worked hard at school, she was making a special effort this time and we wanted to give her every encouragement. It helped, in a way, that I was very tired in the evenings, because it meant that I could spend time with each of the children, listening to any little problems, testing them on homework or perhaps just playing a game of cards with them. I wanted them to know that even though this 'problem' that I had was not going to disappear, we could still lead a reasonably normal family life together without letting it infringe too much on our freedom and ability to enjoy things as a family. Little Gregory provided us with a liberal sprinkling of comic relief. He was only three years old when my PD was diagnosed and he had put his own interpretation on the fact that I sometimes got stuck to the floor. He thought there must be a naughty pixie spreading glue in my path! He had, in his own little mind, thought out a simple solution to this problem and just could not understand why it didn't work. He used to say, 'Walk where I'm walking, Mummy. There's no glue here!'

Three years later, it was unexpectedly brought home to me that I had made a serious miscalculation with regard to Gregory – one that could have had far-reaching results. While I was still in hospital, Peter thought it best to give the girls a brief explanation of my condition and the effects it was likely to produce, concentrating on the positive side, saying that these would happen gradually, and that although there was no cure for it as yet, it didn't come under the category of life-threatening illnesses. However, as Gregory was only three, we decided that he was too young. It was pointless to try to explain the situation to him and therefore we would wait until a later date.

When he was six, he was a happy little boy, always bubbling over with energy and fun. Then, one day I noticed when he came home from school, he was a little less bubbly than usual. He seemed to be uncharacteristically quiet and withdrawn. However, I refrained from asking any questions. I have always enjoyed a close relationship with each of my children and I knew that he would tell me in his own good time. Sure enough, when I was tucking him into bed that night, it all came tumbling out. One of his class-mates had remarked, right out of the blue: 'Your Mum has a disease!' (The tone in which the word 'disease' was pronounced, conjured up in my mind a picture of something disfiguring and very contagious, eg, leprosy!)

'Is it true, Mummy?" he asked. As I looked at his worried little face and the tears shining in his eyes, my heart became heavy with guilt. I felt ashamed and despised myself for not having had the courage to tell him the truth myself, before he heard it from an outsider.

I realised that, although I bitterly regretted what had happened and wished I could have turned back the clock, it had happened and there was nothing I could do to change that. All I could do now was to try to relieve the suffering I had inadvertently caused him. I leaned forward instinctively, scooped him up into my arms and held him close, stroking his hair and rocking him back and forth, at the same time assuring him of my love for him and we remained in this position for some little time until we both felt calmer and able to talk again. Then as I wiped away our tears, I explained what he needed to know, as gently albeit as clearly as I could, in terms he could understand. I took care to stress that it was not a condition that caused people to die, and that I would more than likely be able to carry on as normal for a long time to come. Later, when he had settled down comfortably to sleep, I reflected that perhaps, after all, something good had resulted out of the bad and that by sharing this painful knowledge at this time, an even greater bond had been established between us.

Some years later, Jenny had given me a present of a marble plaque, on which the words of the following prayer were written:

> God, grant me the SERENITY to accept the
> things I cannot change,
> COURAGE, to change the things I can,
> And WISDOM to know the difference.

When I first read it, it put me in mind of the above episode, and since then, it has always had a certain significance for me.

In the Summer of 1988, Peter, Rachel, Gregory and I went on a mini, Euro-Rail trip, making whirl-wind visits to: Switzerland (Lucerne), Italy (Como, Belagio, Venice and Rimini), and France, (Nice, Sanary-sur-Mer), where we stayed in a pre-booked caravan for a week. Bandol, La Grande Motte – an ultra modern town just outside Montpellier – where our very best friends were staying in their caravan on a camp-site and had invited us to drop in on them, which we did, in no uncertain terms. Avignon and finally, Paris, before returning home. We thoroughly enjoyed the venture, but were pretty exhausted by the time we finally arrived home again. The rest of the Summer raced by, and in what seemed like no time at all, we were all back at school. Peter was in the same position as he is now, the Head of a Primary School in Kirkby, Nancy had just graduated, with a Degree in Economics from Durham University, and was about to take a year out to go round the world with her friend, Amanda, who had also been at Durham and had graduated in History. Jenny had also left home, and was working at a Home for the mentally-handicapped in Ormskirk, Rachel was at Sixth-Form College and Gregory was attending a Primary School in the village.

Towards the end of September, my parents came to stay for a few days. My father had not been feeling well and had recently been in hospital. We still had

Nancy, Rachel and Gregory at home in the evenings. This particular evening, we were all in, except Rachel who had gone into Ormskirk with her friends. When I came downstairs after putting Gregory to bed, Peter was in the kitchen. He had started to do the dishes after the evening meal, but I walked in to find him doubled up over the sink, with severe chest pains. When I questioned him, he said he'd had them most of the day and had thought they were probably caused by indigestion. When I heard this, I immediately became concerned and said I was going to phone the Doctor. He didn't argue, which confirmed my suspicions that this was something serious – Peter always did his best to avoid doctors and hospitals. As it was evening, I had to phone the doctor on call, a young man we didn't know. Fortunately, he proved to be very efficient. He examined Peter and said his pain could well be a heart-attack, and that it was imperative that we get him to the hospital as soon as possible. My parents had both gone to bed by this time. While Nancy got a bag ready for Peter to take with him, the doctor phoned for an ambulance. I sat with him, talking quietly in an effort to keep him as calm as possible under the circumstances. We didn't want to disturb my parents because like Gregory, they were now asleep – blissfully unaware of the drama going on around them. There wasn't anything they could do anyway. I needed to go with Peter, of course, and Nancy agreed to stay at home, so that if any of the three 'Sleeping Beauties' awoke, or when Rachel returned, she, Nancy, would be there to supply the necessary information.

The ambulance duly arrived and Peter was transferred, closely followed by me. At that very moment, Rachel turned up on the scene and was hurriedly briefed by Nancy. Rachel made an 'on the spot' decision to come to the hospital and without further ado, climbed into the ambulance and one of the attendants got in with us so he could be with Peter and we set off immediately for the hospital. I was glad to be able to have someone with me after all, and it was good to know that Nancy had taken over the domestic responsibilities, so that I could concentrate wholly on Peter. He was in hospital for ten days. It was a harrowing time for us all, but particularly for Peter himself, not least because the doctors seemed unable to come to a unanimous decision as to whether or not he had suffered a heart-attack. At first he was told that it hadn't been a heart attack and then, a few days later, that decision was reversed! That kind of situation was enough to give him another one! He had to go back into hospital a few weeks later with similar symptoms, and this time the indecisions were the opposite way round.

He had a traumatic time in that kind of ward, because death often struck indiscriminately and without warning. One evening, I was standing in the visitors' queue, waiting to go in to see him. Some of us noticed that just before we were due to go in, there was a sudden flurry of activity, nurses and doctors, with concerned expressions, running around carrying breathing apparatus and other alarming-looking instruments, in and out of the ward. Then a nurse came out and addressed us. She apologised for the delay, but said it had been unavoidable and that we would be allowed in to the ward within the next few minutes. After another ten minutes, the doors were opened and we were admitted to the ward. I was relieved to see Peter sitting up in bed looking alert and pleased to see me, although I was concerned when I noticed the pallor of his skin. He quietly explained the reason for the delay. The man in the bed directly opposite him, who had been admitted for the same reason as Peter, and was soon to be allowed to go home as his general condition had improved, had suddenly suffered a massive heart-attack which had proved fatal. I was shocked by the realisation that it could happen as suddenly as that, even though he was already in hospital and therefore could not have been in a better position to receive professional attention.

Peter was allowed home again after ten days, but he was not considered able to return to work until the following Easter. Life was very difficult for all of us at first. Suddenly, the main source of strength, both physical and emotional, within the family, was now incapacitated and to say that I felt totally inadequate to step into the breach, is the under-statement of the year! There was no way, to my mind, that I would be capable of shouldering the numerous responsibilities that I had always been content to leave to him. Nancy had now more or less decided not to go off around the world, under these circumstances. Her hesitation stemmed not only from concern and a genuine desire to be where she could be of help, but also from a conviction that if Peter were to suffer a relapse, we may be unable to contact her. However, the three of us had a discussion about it and finally made a joint decision that she should go ahead with her plan, because, although none of us knew what the future held, Peter was already beginning to feel better, and we promised to keep her regularly informed, and she, in her turn, undertook to send us an address immediately on each stage of her journey. If, by any chance, we needed to contact her urgently, we would get a message to the nearest *Poste Restante*. I am glad to be able to report, in retrospect, that the urgent contact did not become necessary and she did not, in fact, have to interrupt her travels, which she very much enjoyed.

The first time Peter went back to his own GP for a

check-up, we naturally wanted to hear all that had been said and done, so he duly obliged. Gregory was sitting on the carpet, watching TV and apparently taking no notice of what we were discussing. Peter said he had been debating with the Doctor, which activities he should avoid, and which he could continue in relative safety. He mentioned that the Doctor had remarked that a surprising number of people were not engaged in energetic activity at the time they had died of heart-failure. Then he had said, 'You will probably be sitting in your favourite chair, watching TV when it happens.' At this, a little voice floated up from the carpet, saying anxiously, 'Oh Dad! You'd better sit on the floor!'

About this time I noticed that my medication was beginning to lose its effect, so I made another appointment with my GP to discuss it with her. She said that sometimes it helped to regulate the dose by halving the strength and taking it double the number of times each day – ie, whereas I had been taking four tablets of MADOPAR 250 a day, I would now take MADOPAR 125 eight times a day. As it turned out, I found that six of these tablets was enough for me, so in actual fact, I was taking less than before and getting more satisfaction.

❀

✳

FAVOURITE THINGS

The tranquillity of breaking dawn
Which follows restless night,
So perfect a transition
It must be made by God,
A wild flower newly drench'd
In early morning dew.

A tiny baby gently sleeping
On its mother's breast
New born foals on spindly legs
With shiny flawless coats,
Bright-eyed frisky kittens
With pretty pointed ears
Joyfully springing imaginary foes.

The patterned wings of butterflies
On foliage alighting,
The fragrance of new perfumes
Their interesting aromas pervading the air.

Wild whirling waves crashing on the shore,
Clear and sparkling waterfalls
Splashing over stones
As they wend their merry way.

Yet surpassing all – the Sunshine,
With promise of eternal warmth
Brings out the best in humankind,
Reviving all its spirit.

✳

FRIENDSHIP

She stood alone in isolation
By emptiness surrounded
Her thoughts were grey as a rainy day
Her eyes expressionless.

When his car drove up beside her
And she recognised his friendly face,
The sun began to shine for her,
The warmth at last came flooding in
Refreshing all her senses
With its gentle healing touch.

She knew that he would help her,
Of that there was no doubt,
First, listening attentively
To all she had to say,
Then with sensitive perception
He would smooth the tangled web
And show to her the paths to take
To soothe her anxious fears.

How treasured is this friendship,
Worth more to her than gold
And blest be God who saw her need
For this most generous gift.

Chapter 5

PICKING UP THE PIECES

The variation in my medication worked reasonably well for a number of months, and we were able to carry on a fairly normal family life without having to make too many concessions to 'The Enemy'. My jobs at St Michael's had by this time regrettably come to an end and I was now on the regular supply-lists of Lancashire and Knowsley. There were one or two schools in Skelmersdale for which I supplied fairly regularly. One of these, St Mark's, was the first school I taught in when we returned from Canada. I had a permanent part-time job there, two and a half days a week, in which I was given the task of teaching remedial children, mainly reading. I was a little apprehensive at first, having not had any previous experience in this field, but I soon settled in and found it both stimulating and rewarding. However, by the mid-Seventies, Education found itself in financial difficulties, and teachers were laid off right, left and centre. The part-timers were, of course, the first to go! Lancashire's policy was not to re-appoint when a teacher left for whatever reason. Consequently, when I had to leave to have Gregory, I was not allowed to return to my job, because I had only been teaching with LEA for four years, eight months, rather than the statutory five years, so the job ceased to exist and I had to be content with ordinary supply work. During this period, I did a year's full-time supply at the Catholic Primary school here in Parbold in the Reception class. That is also a time I can look back on with fond memories. I got on very well with the children. They were willing and receptive and I also enjoyed getting to know the parents, whom I found friendly and very appreciative of my efforts. My own personal triumph at this time was that I managed to do the whole year there without having to take a single day's absence.

However, most of the supply work I got was under the Knowsley Education Authority in the Kirkby area, which suited me very well, because I enjoyed working there. In general, I found the Kirkby Head Teachers always very supportive and helpful and their Staff comfortable to work with, which was a pleasant surprise after experiencing and hearing about the treatment of supply teachers in other inner city areas.

When disaster struck, it was totally unexpected. I received a phone-call from Lancashire Education Authority summoning me for interview with the District Education Officer. It transpired that they had received a complaint from a school in that area at which I had recently supplied. They refused to reveal the name of the school, but since the only supply I had recently done for LEA was at two schools, one in Ormskirk and the other in Aughton, where I had done one day in each, respectively, it wasn't hard to guess! I was puzzled as to how the assessment of my ability (or inability) to teach was arrived at, as nobody had come within sight or sound of either classroom, on either day! However, that small detail, obviously irrelevant, and therefore of no consequence to the Powers that Be, I was forthwith issued with an ultimatum: if I wished to continue in their employ, I must agree to one of two alternatives:

(1) Either: I must inform every school in the Authority of the nature of my disability, before I

accepted another job. Or: (2) I must agree to having someone with me in the classroom at all times.

I was not happy with either of these alternatives. All the schools, both in Knowsley and Lancs who called me regularly, knew about my problem and still considered me capable of supply work. However, I was firmly convinced that if Head Teachers who did not know me, were informed of my disability for the first time on the phone, before they had even seen me, their reaction would probably be to say, 'Thanks, but no thanks.' – especially, as it has been my experience to note that the general public is largely ignorant of the symptoms of PD. With regard to the other alternative, the presence of two people in authority in a class of young children, merely serves to confuse them, and they will very likely try playing one off against the other, making things difficult for the two people involved. On account of these difficulties, I was not willing to accept either alternative, but the fact that the LEA were at a loss to understand my reservations came as no surprise to me. The outcome of it was that I found that the whole incident and the way in which it had been conducted, had undermined by confidence to such an extent that I no longer felt competent to carry on teaching. Consequently, I felt that the only thing to do was to take Early Retirement which I proceeded to do with a heavy heart. I had got so much satisfaction out of my teaching career and although I was still relatively young (forty-something), I could think of nothing I could do that would fill the void. How on earth would I fill my days? How would I cope with the inevitable loneliness which naturally follows when there is no challenge left to face, no goal to achieve? I had no answer! All I knew for certain was that I still had plenty to give and that I wasn't yet ready to be thrown on the scrap-heap.

There followed a number of weeks which were some of the darkest and bleakest it has ever been my misfortune to endure. I fell headlong into a deep depression, from which I could not escape. It was as if I had been taking a pleasant walk in the country and had unexpectedly come across an area of treacherous marshland into which I had unwittingly stepped, and now found myself half-submerged and sinking fast, my urgent pleas for help becoming swallowed up in the silence of my surroundings. This horrific mental picture kept returning to my mind, each time more clearly defined, until finally I realised that something had to be done about it. If life had no purpose, what was the use of staying alive? I began to think about it. I went to see a good friend of mine, Michael in Co. Durham, who had given me much help in the past, and who, despite being constantly kept busy with his own work as a Parish Priest, always made an effort to be 'there' for me when I needed him. It was difficult for me to talk about it with a member of my family, they were too closely involved, whereas Michael, not being personally involved, could look on from the side-lines and see the whole problem more clearly. People who are willing and generous with their own personal time are few and far between, like treasures in a field. I was fortunate enough to 'strike gold' some years ago and I have no intention of bartering it at any price.

I travelled to Co. Durham on the train, a journey that took somewhere between three and four hours. Michael met me at the station in Durham and took me back to the house, where we had a light lunch and then settled down to discuss the matter in hand. First, I explained to him what had happened and how I felt about the whole situation. He listened quietly, asking a question here and there to clarify certain things. As I talked, I began gradually to relax and the tension, which had leant so heavily on me throughout the previous weeks, slowly lifted itself from my mind and little by little, gently dissolved into the atmosphere, leaving me feeling calm and unruffled again, ready, as usual, to listen to what he had to say. I could see that he understood how deeply hurt I felt by what I saw as the injustice of the situation and that, being aware of how much I enjoyed teaching, he sympathised with me. However, having done that, he then went on to point out to me that it had now become a *fait accompli* and there was nothing more I could do about it. That phase of my life was now over forever and a new phase was beginning. That being the case, he continued, instead of wasting any more time on sentiments such as anger, frustration and regret, which were negative and futile, why not let them go and concentrate my energies in finding a new occupation to bring some purpose back into my life?

I clearly saw the point of his argument and readily agreed with him. The only problem was that I could think of nothing else I could do other than teach. I had no ideas at all. My mind was a blank. Then Michael had suggested that, since teaching was what I thought I could do best, why not try something on similar lines, but a little less strenuous, ie, a little Private Tuition? Peter had suggested that, but I had rejected it, saying that I would feel too embarrassed when my symptoms showed and that I had no way of knowing in advance if I would feel up to giving the lesson when the time came. We talked more about these particular problems and finally drew up a plan of action for use in dealing with them.

This was easier said than done! I found that my constant and sustained rejection of my symptoms had been so thorough that I had become physically and psychologically incapable of pronouncing the name of the condition. The very thought of it had become so abhorrent to me, that I simply could not bring myself to form the words 'Parkinson's Disease'. If dire necessity insisted that I refer to it, I used to call it my 'problem'. I could see now that if I wanted to maintain a place in society and hold on to what independence I had managed to retain, I had to 'stand up and be counted'. I could no longer hide in a corner, hoping to merge with the scenery. I had to take hold of my courage in both hands and face my disability head-on and challenge it! That was the first thing to do. The second thing I had to do, was to explain the situation to the parents of any would-be private pupils, and state that on account of the erratic way in which the symptoms manifest themselves, I would charge a little less than the going rate.

When I was home again, I took a little while to mull the idea over in my mind, and then decided to give it a try. After all. I had nothing to lose! Accordingly, I put up a notice in one of the local shops and a few days later, a lady came to see if I would take her son, Robert, aged almost nine, for lessons in English grammar. I explained my difficulties to her with more than a little trepidation, half expecting her to stand up and move towards the door, indicating that she had changed her mind. To my surprise, she did not seem in any way perturbed by the revelation and readily accepted the necessary conditions. My faith in human nature was instantly restored! Robert and I liked each other immediately, and got on famously together. He was perfectly capable of doing the work expected of him at school. He had merely 'lost his footing' so to speak in a class of thirty to forty children, and had been unable to grasp certain essential grammar concepts. He improved steadily and I found that I actually looked forward to his regular Tuesday visits. After some months, his little brother, Michael, started to come on alternate Tuesdays, and the arrangement worked so well that after a year they had both caught up in their respective classes. Their mother Anne and I agreed that they could have a break, and then would start again if it became necessary. At this time, I also had three brothers from a different family. The eldest was Gregory's age and came for lessons in French. I had taken French as my main subject at Training College, but because I preferred the Infant age-range, I had never had an opportunity to teach it. I found it an interesting and challenging experience and was greatly encouraged when both Jason's Mum and his teacher told me he had made great strides in his ability to cope in that subject.

As time progressed, so, unfortunately, did the PD and my anxieties and frustrations about it were becoming unbearable, not only for myself, but inevitably, also for those who had to live with me. At this stage, I was having many wakeful nights, caused by chronic cramps which plagued my legs during the night hours, and from which I could get no relief. I had started to write poetry by this time, which I enjoyed doing and which, incidentally, helped a little to express some of the negative feelings which seemed to trample on and annihilate any positive ones attempting to grow. However, although I did not know it at the time, help was now at hand and my lucky day was about to dawn.

I went back to Dr Anderson, my GP, in desperation, and at last, she had the news I had been waiting for – she had found a new Consultant for me. She said she hadn't met him, but she had spoken on the phone with him and was sure he was the type of person I was looking for. He is a Consultant Neurologist at the

Walton Centre for Neurology and Neurosurgery on Merseyside. On my first visit, although I was impressed by the Waiting Area, which was far more comfortable than anything I had seen up till then, but feeling more than a little nervous and apprehensive, I did not take too much notice of my surroundings, except to note that they were a definite improvement on the usual. There was a carpet, rather than lino, the seats and tables were placed in an orderly yet casual manner and they were comfortable to sit on – a far cry from the serried rows of tubular, straight-backed chairs, which were typical of the medical waiting rooms of my experience. There was also a small snack-bar, an easy and pleasant atmosphere, and (best of all) the habitual, nauseous clinical odour was conspicuous by its absence! There was an inner Waiting Room, in which there were magazines and a TV provided. There was also a small play area for little ones, in which, as well as toys, there was also a playpen.

When my name was called out, I followed the nurse, somewhat hesitantly, to the Consulting Room, wondering if Dr Anderson had really understood what I needed. I need not have worried. As soon as I met Dr X, I recognised him immediately as the person I had been searching for so long. I felt at ease straight away. He was courteous, kindly, interested and unhurried. I was also agreeably surprised to note that he possessed that very rare quality of making me feel that, for the time I was with him, there was nothing and no one else on his mind. After giving me a quick examination, he confirmed the diagnosis, and agreed to accept me as his patient. I explained that I badly needed to know more about PD – that I had been bogged down with frustrations and anxieties which I needed to express and discuss with someone who would understand. He seemed to think this was perfectly acceptable, and was amazed to hear that my other Consultant had repeatedly refused to answer my queries. He said he would send me an appointment through the mail at which we could have a good chat. 'Sleeping with the Enemy' had nothing on me, I was not only sleeping with it, I was living and breathing with it as well!

The next surprise was a phone-call from Mary Baker, the Welfare Director of the PDS at its Head Office in London. She turned out to be of a similar disposition to Dr X and I liked her immediately. She told me that both her parents had PD. I remember thinking at the time that this was a strange coincidence. I found her attitude very kind, friendly and sympathetic without being dominant and over-bearing. She explained that there was a branch of the PDS which was wholly concerned with the problems of Early-Onset PD. It was run by a group of these patients, who coined a name for themselves – 'YAPPARS', ie 'Young Alert Parkinson's Partners and Relatives'. They warmly welcomed any other Early-Onset people wishing to join. They do a lot of fund-raising, and four times a year they edit and publish their own magazine called the 'YAPMAG' to which anyone may contribute. A recent copy was sent to me to read and – quite impressed – I decided to join, although I didn't yet feel ready to join a local branch. Mary invited me to get in touch with her whenever I felt the need and I took her at her word! During one of my phone-calls, when I had descended into one of my deep depressions (which I call Darknesses, because that name aptly describes them), she asked me if I had any kind of writing machine. When I replied in the negative, she said she would look into the matter. I imagined she was referring to a second-hand typewriter, and as my condition was now making writing quite an ordeal, ie, it took me over an hour to write a short, simple letter, which when finished, was virtually illegible, I looked forward eagerly to receiving it. Imagine my surprise and delight when, a few days later I received a letter from Roger Jefcoate, whom I learnt was the Technical Advisor for the PDS, enclosing a catalogue of computer/word processors, suggesting which one would probably suit my needs. I wrote a reply thanking him and agreeing with him that the one he had indicated would suit me perfectly. A few weeks later, I took delivery of a brand new computer/word processor – Amstrad PCW-8256. This little machine has become my most prized possession (excluding my children, of course!). It literally provided me with a new and very effective life-line, and has opened whole new vistas of communication and challenge for me. I wrote my first article, entitled: *A Day in The life of Ursula Madden*, which was printed in the YAPMAG. That was the beginning of my new career in writing! I have to date, written a number of articles, most of which have been published in either the YAPMAG or the local press, or both. I have also written about 40-50 poems, of which only a very few pertain to PD. I joined the local WRITER'S CIRCLE and entered their annual competition. I was very encouraged to find that I was awarded First Prize (a silver cup) for my poem entitled *Night and Day*. I had never before won anything for academic achievement, so this was particularly pleasing and satisfying to me.

Perhaps I should mention here – in case some people are wondering – that since becoming Dr X's patient, I was now taking one Selegeline 5 mg and one Amitriptyline 25mg (antidepressant) tablet each day, in addition to the six Madopar 125, which I was still taking, although their effect had been gradually diminishing over the last month. However, on the whole, things had certainly improved dramatically in the last twelve months, with the result that I could now look toward the future in a far more positive frame of mind. I had found a new Consultant, who did me the courtesy of treating me as an equal; who was prepared to do his very best to improve my medical problems; and who would be happy and willing to listen when I needed to discuss my fears and apprehensions with regard to them. The other reason for my new-found optimism, was that I had found a new niche for myself in society through which I could experience once more the joy and satisfaction of 'giving' of myself.

NIGHT & DAY

How subtle are the qualities
That God himself ordained
To change the daytime into night,
And darkness into light.

With what ingenious acumen
And artful expertise
Does Dawn select his colours
To produce a muted blend,
And thus instil a sense of calm
Well suited to a waking world.

Similarly Darkness makes her
Unobtrusive entrance,
Slipping in thru' chinks of light
And introducing shades,
She spreads her mantle cautiously,
Unwilling to disturb
The serenity created by
The fast-departing day.

So swiftly, silently, she moves,
Stepping out on cue,
Gathering in the spoils
Of a newly-conquered world.

THE POWER OF LOVE

I cannot live without your love,
I need it to survive,
To nestle in its safe confines,
Enclosed in all its warmth.

That warmth that has alone the power
To seep into my senses
And fill them with new courage
To face another day.

Without it there can be no light,
And darkness will prevail,
A heaviness of atmosphere,
A smothering of life.

Deprived of you I soon become
A dull and lifeless thing,
A shapeless mass of unformed clay,
Of character devoid.

Yet wrap me in your tenderness,
And nurtur'd by your love,
I can respond with firm resolve
To live again and grow.

Chapter 6

METAMORPHOSIS

Dr X was true to his word and I duly received an appointment to see him one Tuesday morning in January 1992 at 9.30 am. He put me at my ease at once, giving me the impression that his time was at my disposal and that he was genuinely interested in hearing what I had to say and helping me in every way he could. I had never before come across this attitude of sincere concern and singular attentiveness in high-ranking medical staff and I was suitably impressed. I think it worth mentioning, incidentally, that throughout our lengthy discourse, I noticed that he did not once glance at his watch!

I began to feel relaxed and comfortable and gradually found myself sufficiently confident to voice all the qualms and queries about PD that I had been carrying about with me ever since the diagnosis which had changed my life, and consequently that of each member of my immediate family. As a result, at the end of the two-hour session, when I stood up to go, I felt considerably relaxed, refreshed and strengthened. My spirits had risen and my heart was light – light enough to enable me to skip down the corridor for a few seconds, after which I stopped abruptly, remembering that this was a hospital. I half-expected two men to appear out of nowhere, wearing white coats and evil grins, and advance menacingly towards me, carrying a strait-jacket between them!

Anyone reading this, who has had no experience of PD either first-hand as a sufferer, or second-hand as a carer may be interested to know some of the areas we covered in our discussion. Apart from the three main symptoms (Tremor, Rigidity and Bradykinesia), there are a number of other, secondary symptoms which are not necessarily present in every person with this condition. One of the more common of these which I have trouble with, is difficulty in balance, especially moving through doors and around corners (I believe that my own private Hell will be filled with doorways, corners and slopes – there won't be any need for flames, these alone will be sufficient punishment). The severity of these symptoms varies from moment to moment. Another one which plagues me fairly frequently, is Depression. Situations of stress and frustration seem to trigger it and it becomes gradually deeper until I can find something with which to counteract it. One of my mainstays now is the *Amstrad*. A good, hard-working session on it can often be relied upon to lift the 'Darkness' pressing on me and restore me to even-tempered sanity.

Another activity with which I have had a certain amount of success is to get my frustrations out by writing them down. The effectiveness of this tactic depends on the severity of the particular Depression. It is sometimes too far gone to be able to respond. The trick is to concentrate on being 'nice to yourself' in some way. This is by no means as easy as it sounds. In my case, when I am in the throes of a deep Depression, I hate myself and consequently being 'nice to myself' goes against all my instincts and is therefore the very last thing I am inclined to do! Michael, the friend I mentioned earlier in the previous chapter, taught me this ploy. I rejected it at first, but when finally in desperation, I decided to try it in earnest, I was surprised to find it really did work. However, there's no solution that is absolutely fool-proof, that works every time without fail. There will always be, in my experience, certain deeper and more complex moods of dejection and despondency that take a strange-hold on the personality of the individual and firmly resist all attempts to be moved. Anyone who has experienced something of this kind, will know that the only thing to do in this situation, is to remind yourself of all the good things you have going for you (even write them down if necessary), and cling on to these tenaciously, at the same time making a concentrated effort to think positively – blocking out as effectively as you can, any negative thoughts which try to get a foothold. If you do this with real determination, you have every chance of winning through eventually, and I assure you, it is well worth the effort. And that concludes the Sermon for today!

Fatigue is another common symptom with which I have to cope. This problem has increased significantly, in my case, during the last two years. I find it very irritating indeed, because it seems to deliberately choose the most inconvenient of times to strike – e.g. when I am halfway through a basket of ironing, or when I particularly need to do some urgent shopping that I had forgotten earlier; or when I need to keep an important appointment. It starts with a general feeling of weakness, my legs begin to feel shaky and unable to support my weight and a chronic back-ache starts to set in, which increases in severity the more I try to ignore it, until it overwhelms me completely. It leaves me with no alternative but to sit on a chair with a high back and find something to support my legs in a horizontal position. The length of time I have to remain 'marooned' in this position is anybody's guess. I am entirely at the mercy of the *enemy*. My body freezes up and I am unable to move until *it* allows me to do so. It could be within the next hour or I may not regain my ability to walk without difficulty until the following morning! If I lose patience and try to hurry it a little, I only succeed in having to wait even longer. It irks me to be forced to submit to its demands, but I am left with no option. I try to resign myself to it by always having a book handy. This sometimes helps – but if it is in the evening, my eyes quickly get tired with the strain of being under the electric light, and when I have to stop, the feelings of frustration inevitably return.

There are one or two other less common symptoms with which I have had quite a lot of trouble in the past, ie : swallowing difficulties; leg cramps; and insomnia, but these I am glad to say, now seem to have settled down and appear much less frequently. The leg cramps have been greatly relieved by a course of quinine tablets when necessary and a glass of Tonic Water every evening.

The other subject which Dr X and I discussed at some depth, was my anxiety about my constant – and to me – glaring inadequacies in my role as a wife and mother. This is something I have long been conscious of, even before I was diagnosed as having PD. The onset of this particular condition merely emphasised and extended it. There were many things the children seemed to miss out on because I wasn't mobile or confident enough to undertake to get them where they wanted to go independently. I always had to go through the time-consuming and often embarrassing ritual of phoning round our friends and acquaintances to ask for lifts for them. Peter would take them if and when he could (provided that *Old Banger* No. 1, 2, 3, 4, or 5 -- whichever was the current one – was roadworthy at the time) but he rarely managed to get home in time for any early appointments.

Helping with homework, particularly at the top end of the Secondary age-range, was another area in which I keenly felt my inadequacies. English and French were the only subjects in which I could give any real help. In my options year at school, I had to make a choice between Geography and French. I chose French because I enjoyed the lessons and I seemed to have an aptitude for it. Consequently, I left school with virtually no knowledge of Geography and I regard this as a serious handicap. I am totally inept with a map and if you wanted to go to Cornwall and you were foolish enough to ask me for directions, you might very easily end up in Birmingham. My knowledge of the Sciences is negligible and my understanding of Mathematical concepts is by and large non-existent! However, I am at least honest, so I guess that counts for something! It did not help at the time though, and whichever one of the children needed information and explanation at that particular time, was plunged into abject despair by the revelation that their mother was not *Super Woman* after all!! In fact, she was more like *Dopey* of the Seven Dwarfs!

In November '91, Peter and I attended our first National Yapmeet. This is a gathering of registered YAPPARs, from the four corners of the British Isles for a kind of 'think tank' weekend. The venue was the Swallow Hotel in Peterborough. I was very apprehensive and uptight all the way there, wondering what would be expected of me. The only other YAPPARs we had met at that stage, were Hilary and Terry, who lived in Lytham St Annes, about a half-hour's drive away by car. Hilary is the one with PD and it was she whom we met the first time. Terry was at work.

Hilary was the first person I had seen with PD who

was of a similar age and situation to myself and the cheerful and courageous way in which she coped with their inevitable problems was an inspiration to me. We met Terry a few weeks later, when they came to see us in Parbold. He was constantly attentive to her needs, but his calm, casual manner and ever-ready humour, quickly relaxed the atmosphere and put us at our ease, with the result that we thoroughly enjoyed the time we spent with them and looked forward to meeting them again at Peterborough. That first Friday evening was a nightmare for me. It was a considerable shock to me to see all these people with PD all together in one place. Peter and I were amazed at the diversity of the symptoms of the condition. It seemed that no two people were affected in the same way. Even though all PD patients experience several of the more common symptoms, each person's reaction to certain dosages of specific drugs is very individual. Some patients are constantly plagued with Bradykinesis (slowness of movement), others with Dyskinesia (involuntary writhing movements), and others who (like myself) are tormented with both of these at unrelated times, which are impossible to predict. The other two major symptoms, Tremor and Rigidity are usually present in every case of Parkinson's Disease.

I felt claustrophobic, anxious and ill at ease, and would gladly have turned the car around and gone back home, there and then, if Peter had been in a compliant mood. However, having only just completed the journey down, which had not been entirely worry-free, because the car was not in the best of condition, he was not about to agree to my request. He suggested that we stay at least that first night, and make the final decision of whether to stay or go the following morning. A little later that evening, we met up with Hilary and Terry, and also Dave and Val, who make up 2/3rds of the

YAPMAG Editorial Committee. They literally welcomed us with open arms and I very gradually began to thaw out, feeling the real genuine warmth that pervaded – not only that evening but throughout the entire weekend. The next morning at breakfast, we met Janice and Pierre. Janice was the main organiser of the weekend, but I had only spoken to her on the phone, and it was nice to be able to connect the face to the voice. After breakfast, we went back to our room to decide what to do – whether to stay or leave. All things considered, we came to the conclusion that it promised to be less threatening and more interesting than I had previously thought, so our final decision was that because we were already there, we may as well stay and get what we could from it. Looking back now, I would say it was definitely the right decision. Perhaps it would be a good idea at this point for me to give an outline of the procedure of a 'YAPMEET', particularly for those reading this who have never attended one.

It is a kind of 'think-tank' seminar and besides YAP-PARS and their carers, there are also a number of professionals, eg. neurologists, specialist nurses, who work exclusively with PD patients and pharmacists. Friday night is usually spent getting to know people again, and generally having a drink with them and relaxing and exchanging news and views. The following morning after breakfast, we all meet together in the Conference Room to hear a Talk given by Dr Niall Quinn, PDS Medical Adviser, giving us up-to-date information on drug treatment, surgical advances, etc. After this there is usually a coffee-break. There are a number of smaller seminars going on throughout the day and the guests attend whichever ones interest them the most. This is a very individual choice and YAPPARs and their carers may want to attend the same ones together or different ones separately and then discuss later what each has learnt. The option is theirs. That evening there is a Gala Dinner, after which we while away the remainder of the evening drinking and merry-making with old friends and probably some new ones too.

Sunday morning after breakfast, we return to the main Conference Room for another talk by a representative of one or more of the professions. Then we have a coffee-break – and it's back to the Conference Room for a summing-up report on how the weekend has gone. There is then a formal farewell, after which we are left to ourselves to say our individual goodbyes and check addresses and phone-numbers etc. All that remains then is to enjoy an excellent traditional Sunday lunch, after which (or in some cases before which) the guests gradually drift off to start their homeward journey. It is only at that point that my energy suddenly takes its leave of me and I start to disintegrate – fortunately it doesn't matter at this stage, because being one of the lucky ones who do not drive, I can allow myself to relax and spend the length of the homeward journey in a contented haze!

The next time I saw the consultant was April '92 and in the interests of improving things for me, he suggested that I try dropping Madopar altogether for a while and trying a course of Sinemet CR. However, I began very soon after starting it, to have an adverse reaction to it. I seemed to have a great deal of Dyskinesia (involuntary writhing movements) which were accompanied by excessive sweating, which I found very uncomfortable. I stopped it for a short time but when I saw Dr X the following July, we discussed it and decided that perhaps I hadn't given it long enough to 'settle down', so I agreed to continue it for another month. However, as soon as I resumed it, the same reaction followed and for the whole of that month I was plagued with constant, continuous Dyskinesia coupled with excessive sweating. I had no control over it, I got very little sleep and because trying to eat presented such difficulties – I refused to consider allowing myself to be fed, the thought of which, for reasons I cannot explain, was both alarming and abhorrent to me – I quickly lost my appetite. The consultant had mentioned at our last meeting, the possible option of being admitted to the Neurology Centre for assessment and revision of treatment, but on account of my experiences in Salford, I was resolved to avoid this, except in dire necessity. I went again to see him at the beginning of August, and noting the continued deterioration of my condition, he explained the best thing to do would be to admit me into the Walton Centre, in order that he could try different treatments and monitor my reactions at first hand. Recognising that 'dire necessity' had undoubtedly struck, I accepted his judgement without undue anxiety, and agreed to present myself at the Centre as soon as I had been informed that a bed was available.

It turned out that I had to wait another month before I could be admitted and during that time nothing happened to improve my situation. In fact, although we waited till the last minute, we finally had to make the decision to cancel the caravan holiday we had booked in Antibes for the last week in July and the first week in August. Our decision was based on the observation that, if I were sweating so profusely and becoming so exhausted on account of incessant involuntary movement, here, in the mostly mild warmth of an English summer, then I would have had no chance of coping in a caravan in the South of France. It was, of course, a big disappointment for Gregory. He had been looking forward to it and was all geared up to going, but when Peter explained the reasons to him, he accepted it with quiet generosity. One wonderful characteristic that all four of our children have in good measure, is an ability and willingness to rise to the occasion. It comes in very handy, especially at times like this!

The call finally came through via Dr X's secretary on September 1st. She explained that a bed had become available and asked me to check in to Dott Ward the following morning, as near to 9.30 am as possible. I was glad about it now because life was fast becoming unbearable for us all at home. One of the more irksome problems for Peter and Gregory in particular, and for Rachel to a lesser extent (because most of the time she was in Leeds and the other two were also away) was undoubtedly the fact that they could do nothing to alleviate the interminable discomfort and distress which seemed to confront them every time they turned their attention to me. The inevitable strain of it caused irritability and discord between us of a nature that we had not experienced before and were ill-equipped to deal with.

I remember feeling somewhat apprehensive on the journey to the Centre, wondering how it would be, but I did not feel as vulnerable and defenceless as I had done on that previous journey to Salford Hospital. The relationship I had developed with Dr X was on a different plane entirely to the one I'd had with my previous Consultant – which even though I was under his care for several years, was virtually non-existent. I felt confident that I would not be 'talked down to' or ignored and have things sprung on me without warning or explanation. I felt secure in the belief that I could trust the consultant to keep me informed of every procedure beforehand, that he would not easily give up on his quest to find a combination of treatment which would ensure a better quality of life for me, and that he would take time to discuss with me the ensuing results and possible side-effects of the various medications he tried.

The first thing I noticed about the Walton Centre, was that a united and concerted effort was made to keep the emphasis on the positive rather than the negative. The sense of it was so real to me as to be almost tangible, as it spread through the building like a fragrant aromatic bouquet and even at that early stage, it soothed my frayed nerves and emanated a sense of security and calmness so that the small tight knot of tension which had grown inside me, was dispersed and I began to feel better. This was so different from the reception I had been given on arrival at Salford – or indeed, any other hospital.

The receptionists who filled in the various forms for me (on account of my state of health I was incapable of having the necessary control over my hands to be able to write legibly) was pleasant and friendly – and so too I found when I got up to Dott Ward, were the nurses. The rooms on this ward were mostly either single-bedded or four-bedded. I was directed to one of the latter and the bed which had been allocated to me was on the inner side of the room and next to it was a large window over-looking the main corridor of the ward, which was busy for a large part of the day with people coming and going about their business, not only doctors and nurses but patients and visitors also. During my stay there, which turned out to be longer than had been expected due to certain small complications caused by side-effects, I frequently got a wave and a smile from someone passing by. Sometimes, they would even pop in for a few words. I made several new friends this way, with whom I still correspond regularly. I will come back to them a little later.

Soon after I got into bed, a youngish lady doctor

came to examine me. She was very pleasant and did not seem to mind answering any queries I put to her – that is, those she felt confident with. Those that did not come into this category she advised me to put to Dr X (under whom she was working) when I next saw him, which, of course I had every intention of doing. She said he would probably give me a chance to settle in, and would be in to see me later in the week. I was to see quite a lot of this lady during my stay and I found her friendly equanimity very soothing, especially at the times when my symptoms were particularly obnoxious. The colleague with whom she worked in close proximity, I did not take to as readily. It wasn't that he was harsh or unkind and he appeared reasonably competent. It was just that he was always disinclined to listen and too ready to jump in and finish my sentences for me instead of waiting for me to finish them myself. This habit of his, although I don't suppose he deliberately intended to be forceful or discourteous, irritated me because, after all, how could he possibly know what was in my mind better than I did myself?

The consultant, as I had been told to expect, came in to see me in the latter part of the week. As, at the time of his visit, I happened to be in the throes of a very distressing bout of Dyskinesia, I was particularly relieved to see him, knowing he would do all he could to ease the problem, not only in the long-term but also in the short term. He explained to me that the first thing to ascertain was whether this problem was being caused by the drug, Sinemet CR, or whether it was a direct result of a sudden escalation of the progression of PD. He said the only way to be sure, was to cancel all the medication I had been taking, for a full twenty-four hours and observe what happened.

This having been carried out, the first thing of which

I became aware was the immediate cessation of Dyskinesia. This was such a wonderful relief to me, it was like a miracle. Just to have normal control over my movements, and to be able to eat without it being a major challenge was absolute bliss! However, as the hours without any medication increased, all my movements gradually slowed down until finally they stopped altogether and I became 'frozen' (totally immobile) and incapable of doing anything for myself. I had to resort to accepting assistance for the most mundane activities, ie. eating, drinking, taking a bath, going to the wash-room and the most basic of all – turning over in bed. I felt exasperated when I discovered that I was only able to read (one of my favourite pastimes) for a few minutes at a time because my hands kept dropping the book and losing the page. One of the nurses would come and fix my pillows behind me so that I could sit up comfortably, but I would soon begin to feel myself slipping and the next time the poor girl came in to the room, she would have to do them all over again. I was impressed that not one of the nurses ever complained to a patient about being summoned. No matter how many times they were called, they always came with a pleasant smile and a genuine willingness to help. It hardly came as a surprise to me, therefore, that on being asked by me separately, if they liked their job, the answer was, for the most part, an enthusiastic affirmative.

One day, about a week after my arrival, the Library Lady arrived, with her helper (who was never given a chance to help!), and her trolley-load of ancient, dog-eared books, and offered to lend one to me. At first, as I failed to be captivated by any of the titles, I politely declined. At this point, determined not to emerge as the loser, she immediately launched into a long eulogy on the merits of books in general, and hers in particular, which, although it did nothing to alter my opinion, did achieve its purpose in a sense, by persuading me that the only way to regain tranquillity, was to capitulate, so I finally agreed to take one on her own recommendation. Satisfied that she had achieved her purpose, she walked to the end of the bed so that she could copy my name off the record sheet.

Doing her best to appear efficient, she announced in a loud voice: 'It's Mrs Parkinson, isn't it dear?' Weary though I was, this had the effect of reducing me to a fit of giggles, as I protested that it was Mrs Madden. Obviously concluding that I was attempting to ridicule her, she became annoyed and said in a voice of strong disapproval: 'Well, it says Parkinson on this form', in a tone which left me in no doubt that she suspected me of lying. Seeing that I was in no mood to behave sensibly, she gave up trying to get any sense out of me and marched out with her trolley wearing an affronted expression on her face. When she returned to collect the book, she appeared to have forgotten the incident, so I decided not to risk reminding her by ordering another book.

The selecting and grouping of a combination of medication for PD is a difficult and time-consuming process. The symptoms are so variable that each individual patient must be considered separately. What is right for one is not necessarily right for another. Also to find the correct dosage is crucial. To err on either side could produce symptoms with which the individual cannot cope, eg, insufficient doses can cause an increase Bradykinesia (slowness of movement), or Dyskinesia (involuntary movement) can result if a particular dose is too high. In my own case it took a number of weeks of trial and error to strike the right balance, because I also had to contend with side-effects such as cramp, nausea and sleeplessness. As my main objective in writing this book is to highlight the social rather than the medical aspects of the condition, I will not go into detail here. However, in case anyone is interested, I will include a list of my present medication at the back of the book.

One day, towards the end of my sojourn, the other doctor, who was studying my case together with the lady doctor, sent a message enquiring if I would mind if he brought some students in to see me. I assented, after some slight hesitation, and he duly arrived a few minutes later with a group of about ten students in tow. He explained to them that I had PD, and asked them if they could discern any secondary symptoms. There was a few minutes silence while they all searched in the nether regions of their minds to come up with something. They didn't seem to be having much success until one of them suddenly came out with the very one I did not expect or appreciate. She ventured hesitantly: 'Mask-like face?' My response was immediate and automatic, 'I love you too!' I said with a rueful smile. It had the instant effect of diffusing the tension in the atmosphere and producing spontaneous laughter, as they allowed themselves to relax and enjoy the moment. I hoped they left the ward in a more cheerful frame of mind than they had entered it.

I spent eight weeks in the Walton Centre and in terms of medical care I couldn't fault it. The nurses and doctors on Dott ward were, without exception, some of the most hard-working, capable and dedicated people I have ever come across. When I left, I reflected that not only had my physical condition vastly improved, which I largely attribute to the skill and infinite patience of Dr X, but a great upsurge of spiritual growth had taken place, enabling me for the first time to start taking control of my own life. The whole episode had been a very fruitful experience for me, in that it had revealed hidden depths in me which, if explored, could perhaps turn me from a crawling, colourless caterpillar to a soaring, multi-coloured butterfly.

EMERGENCE

Emerging, somewhat breathless
From the devastating darkness,
I find myself incapable
Of feeling human warmth.

My small reserves of energy
Have fast become exhausted
In my weak and feeble struggles
'Gainst the constant trials of life.

My God, I do entreat you
Do not avert your eyes,
Do not refuse to give your aid
To one whom you have made.

Stretch out your hand toward me
Let me feel its strength in mine,
And revive my downcast spirit
With the fragrance of your Love.

IN PRAISE OF TIME

How brief the time
God gives to us
In this short life of ours.
So little time
To give our love
So little time
To care.

So short a time to notice
How others live their lives,
To share their grief
And happiness,
To comfort and rejoice.

O would we could
Be given more,
A space in which to stand,
To contemplate,
With measur'd thought
The way the earth revolves.

If so, perhaps
We could begin to see
Where we fit in,
Why we received
The gift of Life
Why we were born at all.

Yes, Time is of the Essence,
T'is such a precious thing
Appreciate it while we can
Too soon shall it be gone.

Chapter 7

NEW HORIZONS

Apart from the professionals, I met many lovely people – both patients and visitors alike – who made me feel 'wanted' because they seemed to go out of their way to come and talk to me and sometimes they asked to read some of my poetry. Often they wanted to share their anxieties about the condition of loved ones, whom they were visiting and felt the need of a sympathetic ear.

Others were patients themselves and were worried about how their families were coping without them or, in the case of patients who lived alone, how they would manage when they left hospital. They seemed to single me out and take me into their confidence. I had never been in this role before and I felt privileged to have been chosen. I realised that they must have seen a quality in me of which I had been hitherto unaware. It did wonders for my self-image!

One lady came in one day specifically to tell me how much she admired me. When I asked her the reason, she said that she passed the window two or three times a day in order to visit her son and when she glanced in my direction, I was always smiling. I was amazed that such a simple natural reaction could have made such an impression. A small group of people still keep in touch with me by phone and mail and I am always glad to hear from them.

Ruth, an attractive girl in her mid-twenties was at the hospital day and night for the first two or three weeks after I had been admitted. There was no sign of illness or injury, so one day when we happened to be walking back along the corridor at the same time, she seemed friendly and after we had exchanged greetings, I told her my reason for being there and asked her why she was there. She explained that she wasn't a patient herself, but her husband, Keith, who was about the same age as herself, was dying of a brain tumour. His parents and his twin sister used to come in every day and as I got to know them better I realised that the lady who remarked about my smiles was actually Keith's mother. I found it incredible that someone who had to cope with that kind of tragedy in her family could be moved by a stranger's smile and perhaps even derive some solace from it. It was an awe-inspiring thought!

Ruth and Keith had two small children, a boy and a girl, who were being cared for by relatives while Ruth was at the hospital. It was doubly sad, because Keith had had the same problem a couple of years earlier. At that time he had had an operation and had made a full recovery. Then in the summer of '92 he began to get bad headaches again and returned to the Centre for investigative surgery. Unfortunately, this time when the surgeons took a look, they found another growth which was so extensive that nothing could be done. He died towards the end of my second week. Two or three days beforehand, I lent a compilation tape to Ruth and she said she would play it in Keith's room so that they could enjoy it together. He was unable to talk at this stage but he could listen and register his reactions with his eyes. When she returned it to me the following day, she reported that he was having a slight remission and had actually been able to talk to her. He died that same evening, so it was nice to think they had had an opportunity to share one last thing. I greatly admired

Ruth's resilience and courage for the way that she put her life back together again and started anew with her two little ones. Her serenity was remarkable. We still keep in touch by letter and occasionally she finds time to come and visit me.

Elsie, a gentle sweet little lady in her seventies, was brought in from another hospital for tests because she was unable to walk, having suffered a fall at home sometime previously. She was offered an operation to try to repair the damage, but she was warned by the surgeon that it was long and serious, and that he could not guarantee that it would work. It had to be her decision, but on being pressed for his opinion, the surgeon replied that he wouldn't recommend it. After some slight hesitation she decided against taking the chance and was subsequently returned to the hospital from which she had come. Even though we only shared a room for a few days, we took an instant liking to each other and formed an attachment. Some months later, I received a note from her niece, who had by then returned to her home in Australia, on which was written the name and address of the Nursing Home in which Elsie now lives, in Liverpool I visit her as often as I can, which tends to be about every six weeks or so. I wish it could be more often, but at least it's better than nothing. I will always remember the surprise and pleasure that registered on her face, the first time I went to see her. I could not have wished for a better welcome.

Susan is another friend I made in the Walton Centre. Her mother was brought in having suffered what appeared to be a serious stroke and was very ill for several weeks. The family lived on the Isle of Man and because Esther was so ill and her life was in the balance, her husband and family of three girls and a boy were given temporary accommodation in the nurses' home. They were all grown-up and had jobs to go to, but there were always at least two of them continuously at the bedside, talking to Esther – willing and encouraging her to bring her mind back from wherever it had gone. When I was slowly regaining my ability to walk again, one or other of the staff would take me for a walk round the corridor. I used to wave to them as I went past their window, because their constancy reminded me of my own family.

I gradually got to know Susan and her sister Joanne and they used to come and see me most days for a chat. Despite their fears and worries about their mum, they were always friendly and good-humoured. Finally, just before I left, their devotion and perseverance was rewarded. Esther began, at last, to show the first signs of recovery. From then on, she has been making slow but steady progress. They returned home to the Isle of Man and Susan writes regularly to let me know how things are going. I look forward to her letters.

Jenny is another lovely person connected with the Centre. She was not a patient or a visitor. She is a 'project nurse' which – she told me – involves teaching the staff how to use the computer. She does not have to wear a uniform, except at certain times when extra staff are needed to man specialist areas, eg, the Intensive Care ward. I first noticed her because she used to pass by my window at least once a day. She's a pretty, little blue-eyed blonde, with a remarkable talent for choosing her wardrobe to suit her colouring and set off her slight frame to advantage. Her clothes were always well co-ordinated and a perfect fit. Even before I got to know her, her appearance, especially in those first harrowing weeks when side-effects were making life difficult for me, never failed to cheer me, making me realise that there was a world outside the confines of the Medical Centre, that would once more

become a part of my life at some stage in the not too
distant future.

One day, when I was practising walking on my own
and had got glued to the floor outside the wash-rooms
on my way back into my room, she stopped to ask if I
needed help, I took the opportunity to tell her about
the effect she had on me. She proved to be as pleasant
as she looked and we became firm friends. She loved
reading my poetry and asked if she could have copies
of it. We were both intrigued by the fact that she was
already doing me so much good without even being
aware of it!

I was a little taken aback to find that people seemed
to be actively seeking out my company. This was not
something I was familiar with and I found it hard to
believe. When I was growing up, I had not found it
easy to make friends, and I tended only to have one
special one at a time. I was somewhat quiet and withdrawn – and the fact that I was inclined to stammer
when nervous or excited did little or nothing for my
self-esteem! I therefore resolved to put these new-
found friendships to the test. Although I had
exchanged addresses and telephone numbers before I
left hospital, I decided not to attempt to make any con-
tacts first. They might have felt obliged to reply in that
case and that wouldn't have provided me with the confirmation I needed. I was very gratified when within
three weeks of returning home, each one of them had
renewed contact with me, either by phone or letter!
Two extra ones whom I had only met two or three days
before I had left, also wrote to me. One of them, an
elderly gentleman who painted in water-colours as a
hobby, sent a picture of the canal at Parbold which he
had done especially for me!

My family were also very attentive throughout my
hospitalisation. During the early part of my stay,

Rachel was back in Leeds, preparing to go to Spain, where she was required to spend the third year of her four-year Degree course. Although she must have been very busy, she somehow found time to visit me several times a week. Even though she had to use public transport – and on account of delays in train connections, it would take her the best part of the day to get there, not to mention the cost – she never hesitated. She would leave Leeds at about 10.00 am or earlier and only arrived at Walton at about 3.00 pm. Then she would usually stay until about 7.00 pm when Michael, her boyfriend would come over in the car and take her back. I was agreeably surprised to find that the staff were pleasantly accommodating where visiting was concerned. Visitors were allowed to come and go more or less as they pleased, a point greatly appreciated by both visitors and patients alike.

Rachel proved to be a great source of strength and comfort to me at that time, all the more so because Peter and Gregory were unavailable during the day and Nancy and Jenny both lived and worked down south, although they did what they could by keeping me posted. Rachel would know immediately if I were anxious or upset and she would talk the problem through with me until I felt better and able to cope with it. There were lighter moments too, when we would regale each other with amusing anecdotes. On the day before she left for Spain, Dr X readily gave permission for me to go out for a meal with her in Southport together with Peter and Gregory. We very much enjoyed it, although the presence of Nancy and Jenny was sadly missed.

Jenny and her boyfriend Paul managed to arrange a visit to the Centre just before Rachel left for Spain, so we were able to spend an afternoon catching up on each others' news. Just before they left, Paul went out

and came back with a lovely bouquet of seasonal flowers, so I had something tangible with which to remind
myself of that day.

Nancy and her boyfriend Adrian went on a pre-
arranged holiday to India for three weeks. They sent
an endless supply of interesting post-cards, in which
every inch of available space was written on! Peter
drove over most evenings with magazines, some of
which had been sent by friends who, for one reason or
another, were unable to make the journey themselves.
I appreciated his efforts, particularly as I was aware of
how hard he worked at school. He must have been very
tired in the evenings, yet he was always cheerful and
more often than not, had something amusing to tell
me. Gregory would sometimes accompany him, unless
he had a previous commitment or some homework to
do. One evening, when they came together, Peter had
bought a *Liverpool Echo* on his way in. Having greeted
me enthusiastically and established that my health
was improving, they promptly sat down, one on either
side of me, divided the paper between them and settled
down to a good read, leaving me, sitting between them,
staring into space and talking to myself.

When Nancy and Adrian returned from India, Peter
asked if I might go home for the weekend and permission was granted. I have to admit to having some mis-
givings about the prospect, because I still needed assistance with most necessary activities, and I did not
want to impose too much on their generosity. However,
I allowed myself to be enthusiastically persuaded by
Nancy and Peter, neither of whom were prepared to
take no for an answer. They insisted that everything
would be okay, and so it was, thanks to them. Nancy
was constantly on hand to help with anything and
everything. Nothing was too much trouble and she and
Peter put all their energies into making the weekend

an enjoyable and satisfying experience. Nancy gave us a lively, colourful and at times, hilarious account of her Indian holiday, including some hair-raising incidents that had inevitably occurred along the way. For example, when in her hurry to board a moving train (which happened to be the last one that day), she lost one of her shoes irretrievably when it slipped off her foot and fell down the space between the edge of the platform and the train! There's never a dull moment in Nancy's life. Adrian, at the time, was in an even more precarious position, being behind her and desperately trying to cling on while the train gathered speed. As he was hauled aboard by numerous helping hands, he scraped his leg and it started to bleed. Once he was safely aboard, he started to search in his bag for something with which to staunch the flow and cover the cut. When he glanced up, he noticed that a railway worker was waving an oily rag in his direction, which he hastily but pleasantly declined!

After I left the Walton Centre, I maintained the considerable improvement in mobility that the consultant had secured for me. The mornings were remarkably good. I enjoyed two and a half hours (from 9.00 am to 11.30 am) of normal, uninterrupted movement every morning without fail. It was so good that I could rely on it – something I had not been able to do for a very long time. Gregory, observing this phenomena one day, remarked that no one seeing it would know I had PD and they might question my right to an Orange Badge, which I had only just got. He had a good point!

Now that I was back home again, I needed another project into which I could immerse my energies in order to avoid too much frustration. I had enjoyed my stint of private tuition, but that had finished at the end of the Summer term and I felt the need for a change. It was Anne, Robert's mother, who first suggested that I write a book about my life with PD. I didn't see much point in doing it at first as I knew there were already several books of similar ilk.

However I didn't reject the idea outright. I kept it in my mind for a few weeks giving it a few minutes thought from time to time. Gradually, it occurred to me that although other people had written about it, both from an autobiographical and from a medical point of view, no one, to my knowledge, had yet focused on the effects it had on the family as a whole, and as separate individuals. I am talking now of just an ordinary family, engaged in ordinary, everyday activities, and having to adapt to all the changes and inconveniences that a progressive, degenerative disease imposes on them, both collectively and separately, when it occurs in one of their number – in this case the wife and mother.

The more the idea grew, the more interested I became. I wrote 'THE DIAGNOSIS' (Ch. 2) in a rush of enthusiasm, which was promptly followed by a period of disillusionment which inevitably brought my writing to a standstill for a few months. Then, Brenda, a close friend of long standing, came across some of my poetry one day, and was quite captivated by it! Delighted and encouraged by her reaction, I tentatively brought up the idea of the 'book'. She was immediately interested and asked to read 'THE DIAGNOSIS'. Having read it, she seemed convinced that there was a need for it and that I should continue with it. When I hesitated, she suggested that I send each section to her as it was finished so that we could discuss it. We have kept to this arrangement throughout, and I have derived tremendous help and encouragement from it. Her involvement has been invaluable to me. It's interesting to note that her husband and family have gradually become infected by her enthusiasm so that they have also begun to read it. Dr X, Dr Anderson (my GP) and Mary Baker

(Welfare Director of the PDS) have read the first five chapters and have kindly implied that they are looking forward to reading more, as has Peter Rogan, Headteacher of St Michael's Primary School, Kirkby. I am deeply appreciative of the wonderful support I have been given in this venture, particularly by these professionals, who clearly demonstrate in their daily lives their total understanding and commitment to what is referred to, somewhat glibly by some, as the 'Caring Profession'.

When I had to give up teaching, I remember someone saying, 'Don't worry! when God closes one door, He opens another!' I took no notice at the time, but I wonder now if there may be some truth in that! If I had not had to end my teaching career, I might never have discovered a penchant for writing poetry etc, in which case I should have missed some very happy hours on the word-processor. Maybe I'll even write a successful novel one day!

In order to be able to cope at least adequately with the aggravations of PD – whether you are a carer, a patient, or just a friend, who occasionally comes into contact with it – there are two essential characteristics you will need in good measure. The first is determination and the second is a sense of humour.

§

I have just returned form Peterborough, where I attended the first 'International Yapmeet', which was held from the 13-15th May at the Swallow Hotel. Peter was unable to come with me because of a prior engagement, so Nancy stepped in to accompany me. The theme was: *To Hell With Parkinson's*. It was all that that implies and more besides! One professional's closing words were: "If I had been asked ten years ago if a cure would be found for PD I would have said 'no'. If I were asked today, I would say 'probably'."

What better note of optimism on which to finish?

UTOPIA 2

To be at peace with God and self,
To have no grievance with the world,
No quarrel with our fellow-men,
How enviable a state!

Yet there is no place for Envy
In a newly-ordered world,
No room for petty jealousies,
Disharmony and greed,
We have to rise above ourselves
And set our standards high,
Forget our baser instincts
And look to better things.

The richness of true Justice,
The glow of tender Love,
The warmth of Generosity,
The confidence of Hope.

If there be essential goodness
In each and every soul,
The sunshine of content shall rise
Upon a new horizon.

Chapter 8

A FEW EXTRA RAINBOWS

AUTUMN'S LEGACY

The summer sun is on the wane
And song-birds cease to sing,
The gentle breeze expands in strength,
The sky is clothed in grey.

The trees proclaim their splendour
In yellow, red and gold,
Their varied colours changing
As daylight starts to fade.

Alas, their beauty does not last,
Deprived of crucial warmth,
Unable to endure the loss
They shrivel up and die.

Likewise, the Spirit withers
Through lack of human warmth,
It needs new seeds of Hope
To be implanted at its core.

Then shall it gleam with healthy glow,
And radiate with life,
Its very depths by faith restored
And courage fortified.

THE BRIDGE

Walking through this leafy glade,
I revel in tranquillity,
My thoughts transcend from worldly cares
And peace is all around me.

The sunshine filters through the trees,
And as I pause absorbing warmth,
A rustic bridge comes into view.

And now a silent question forms
Within my cleared mind,
Should I attempt to cross the bridge
The more delights perhaps to find?
Or should I stay here
Where I am
And savour what I have?

How many more have trod this path
And faced this same dilemma?
Did they decide to cross the bridge
In search of further treasure?
Or did they opt like me to stay,
Afraid of what they'd find?

Perhaps one day
I'll cross the bridge
If courage can be found
Till that day dawns
I shall remain
And keep what I have thus far gained.

THE STRUGGLE

*The sun was declining
In a haze of reddish hue,
Its image reflected
In the waters below.*

*She walked towards it barefoot,
Hesitant, unsure,
Seeking warmth and reassurance,
Not knowing where it lay.*

*She gazed across the sunlit sea,
And longed for him to come
And offer her his gentleness,
To show that he still cared.*

*He'd always been a part of her,
And now that he was gone,
No-one else could give to her
The solace that she craved.*

*'Come back', she pleaded silently
From out her tortur'd soul,
'Restore my withered spirit,
And banish solitude'.*

*In time she felt tranquillity
To flow, as life's blood
Thru' her veins
Rejuvenating her,
And though she could not see him,
She knew him to be there,
Sharing with her in her pain,
Thus lightening the load.*

*She need no longer be afraid,
For warm affection always wins
'Gainst isolation's lethal grasp.*

*This calming influence prevails,
And for a while she is at peace.*

❀

Just Desserts

❀

❀

After a satisfying but tiring day, teaching, we drove into Liverpool city centre, searching for a parking space, which we eventually found. Having had PD (Parkinson's Disease) for eleven years, I have discovered that its most debilitating feature is that the varied forms in which it manifests itself are totally unpredictable. Therefore, I can make no preparation for them: ie, at any moment, from behaving in a perfectly normal manner, I can find myself either entirely incapacitated, unable to move in any direction, or alternatively, plunged into a weird 'dance', my limbs jerking uncontrollably in all directions – rather like a puppet whose strings have become entangled!

On this particular evening, having left the car, I suddenly found myself in the former state, ie, completely immobile. Peter, my husband, tried to propel me forward, to no avail. My feet were firmly glued to the floor. All that happened, was that I lost my balance, falling forward full-length onto the pavement. Peter, not expecting this, tripped over my legs, landing on top of me.

We were both a little surprised that no-one stepped forward to offer us any assistance. However, we realised the reason for this when, struggling to our feet, we glanced up. There in front of us, emblazoned in lights, were the words: *Yates' Wine Lodge*!

❀

English Speaking Board Exam. Grade S (1992)

Talk by Gregory Madden

❀

❦

Hello! Today I will be giving a talk on Parkinson's Disease.

You may be wondering why a boy of my age would be interested enough to research and prepare a talk on a disease which is relatively unknown among my generation.

There are two reasons for this:

Firstly, I feel that people should become more aware of this, although not fatal nor contagious, but, nevertheless, frustrating and disabling condition.

Secondly, my interest extends to a personal level, as my mother was diagnosed as having Parkinson's Disease shortly after I was born.

Parkinson's Disease is a chronic, degenerative movement disorder. It is the result of a deficiency of a normally occurring chemical in the brain. This chemical is called 'Dopamine'. Roughly, its job is to send messages from one nerve-cell to another. PD (Parkinson's Disease) occurs when approximately 80% of these cells have died.

There are many symptoms connected with PD, but there are three main ones: tremor, rigidity and slowness of movement. My mother first became suspicious when she noticed a fairly constant tremor in her right hand. There are many other secondary symptoms including: poor balance, fatigue, general weakness and loss of dexterity. However, a patient will not necessarily suffer from all of these. PD is most often identified when two or three main symptoms are present. These generally increase during times of stress. Movement is seriously affected. It can take a great deal of conscious effort to

do what most people do automatically. This is exhaust-
ing.

The condition is helped by a variety of medications.
However, what suits one patient doesn't necessarily suit
another. Success is achieved after much trial and error.
My mother generally takes a pill called 'MADOPAR',
although she is currently experimenting with another
one 'SINEMET CR (ie, controlled release). Also services
such as Physiotherapy, Occupational Therapy, Speech
Therapy and Aromatherapic Massage can be helpful. A
healthy life-style and a positive attitude help immea-
surably.

I have known about my mother having PD since I
was about 6 years old, but it is only in the last two to
three years – as it has progressed to a significant level –
that I have begun to realise the fact that she does have
this particular condition, and it will worsen and it will
affect me! As my three older sisters have now left home,
during the next few years I am sure that I will play an
important role in assisting her to cope with everyday
life. Thankfully, it is progressing relatively slowly, but
others are not so fortunate.

At present, there is no known cure for Parkinson's
Disease. However, scientists are applying the newest
research techniques to the study of this puzzling condition.

❀

�֍

The Queue

�֍

❊

Christmas, in our house, usually starts at about 7.00 pm on the 24th December. The main reason for this, is that I refuse, on principle, to take any serious notice of 'High Street Tinsel-Time' and all its accompanying hysteria, before the beginning of December at the very least. I take up a dignified stance on the side-lines, observing the proceedings with a detached air, while firmly resisting any attempts by over-zealous shop-keepers, to draw me in. It happens every succeeding Christmas and this last one was no exception. It invariably gets to the middle of the month before I start making any serious effort to begin the 'necessaries'. Usually, it works out alright, and I am still able to get what I intended to get – or, if not quite that, then something very similar which serves the purpose equally well. However, this year I finally got my comeuppance having, as usual, deluded myself into believing that most people would have already done their shopping, and therefore queues would be vastly reduced. How wrong can you be? They were still bursting at the seams and remained so, right up until the last available moment on Christmas Eve. Consequently, many of the late shoppers in Wigan and Southport, were able to go home with a ready-made excuse as to why they were so late back. I could almost see them relating – half-amused, half-irritated – to their wide-eyed, hungry and disgruntled families, the story of how, '...this stupid woman further up in the queue steadfastly refused to move either up or out of the queue, insisting that her feet were stuck to the floor! Did you ever hear such nonsense! Several of us had seen her a few moments before, behaving perfectly normally. Honestly, the lengths that some people will go, to get to the front of a queue is incredible! Of course I blame the Social Services. They shouldn't allow those people out of their institutions on their own. They can't cope and they're a menace to serious shoppers.'

Feeling somewhat deflated and highly frustrated, I made my long, slow journey home, wistfully wishing that my Fairy Godmother would get her act together and turn me into a beautiful Cinderella instead of into a pumpkin!

When I got home, I too related the story, just as it had happened, to my own family. They listened with genuine interest, and that subtle blend of sympathy and humour which seems to be a genetic trait in our family. As I gradually found myself able to unwind and relax in the warm, comforting atmosphere which their response had created, and laugh with them at the amusing situation their comments conjured up in our minds, I was reminded of the words of a song from Andrew Lloyd Webber's *Aspects of Love* entitled 'Love Changes Everything', and I sent up a silent prayer of thanksgiving to God in appreciation of all that I had. After all – isn't *Giving* what Christmas is all about?

Love can turn your world around
And that love will last forever!

❀

93

❁

A Day To Remember

❁

❀

Saturday, September 4th dawned just like any other day, and when I awoke at 7.00 am, its significance did not immediately register with me. However, a minute later it came to me. It was to be Jenny's Wedding Day! The day for which we had been preparing for a year had finally arrived. I didn't know whether to laugh or cry. It was the first time we had ever hosted such an occasion and it had loomed as a tremendous responsibility. Jenny is our second daughter.

The fact that I have had PD (Parkinson's Disease) for twelve years inevitably complicated things, ie, I could not be relied upon to be able to get to places such as the Wedding Hire Shop alone. I would have to wait for Peter to find the time in his very busy schedule to drive me there, which at times, could be frustrating for both of us. The three girls presented further difficulties, by the fact that they all lived separately, Jenny in Hertford, Nancy in Luton and Rachel in Spain, and as you can imagine, getting them together for fittings, alterations and 'any other business' became a feat of gigantic proportions! Many times during the last year I have literally, longed to be an ostrich so that I could just bury my head in the sand and let them all get on with it!

In the beginning, I resorted to 'letting my fingers do the walking' and, provided I could stagger into the living room with the Yellow Pages – and in so doing negotiate the inevitable *Early Morning Obstacle Course*, without incurring too many bruises – the rest was easy. All I had to do then was to sit on the floor, look up the item in question and pick up the phone to make the necessary enquiries. That was how I found the Wedding Dress Hire Shop, which provided every-thing for the Bride, Groom, Best Man, Bridesmaids, Father of the Bride and the two ushers. By the same method – all of which proved highly successful – I also ordered the Wedding car, the place to hold the recep-tion, the Wedding cake, and the evening Disco, .

As the final few weeks turned into days, it became apparent that the only thing that had not been organ-ised was the outfit for the mother of the Bride! I offered to attend the wedding clad solely in the under-wear which had been purchased especially for the day, and was particularly pretty, but the idea was hastily quashed on the pretext that I might inadvertently steal the lime-light from the Bride!

I was finding it increasingly difficult to find any-thing suitable in the shops, mainly because they were in the process of changing their stock from Summer-wear to Autumn-wear and consequently I couldn't even find anything to try on. Finally, two Saturdays before the wedding date, Peter – who has a talent for finding clothes that look as though they might have been made for me – spotted a particular suit which had been delivered only that morning to 'Principles' in Southport, and he told me to forget the colours I had been favouring (pink or purple) and try this new colour – mustard. I was a little dubious, having never worn that colour before, but I agreed to try it on. As soon as I looked in the mirror, I was sold! It was of a style I liked, a neat little jacket and a straight skirt, the colour suited me and – most important of all – it was a perfect fit.

So now the day was upon us and there was no escape! I take my first medication at 8.00 am, and then I have to wait for it to take effect – usually about half-an-hour to three-quarters – so I usually get up around 8.30 am. The Wedding Ceremony was to begin at 3.00 pm, so there was plenty of time. During the interval, between taking the medication and getting up, I mentally checked everything by ticking each one off an imaginary list in my mind – clothes, flowers, hair-appointments, accessories, car, cake, etc. Everything seemed to be well in hand. The lady from the flower-shop was delivering the flowers (unlike the night-mare of our own wedding, when Peter, all dressed up in his morning suit, hitched a lift in a lorry to fetch the flow-ers – but that's another story).

Jenny and Paul had travelled up from their flat in Hertford the day before, bringing with them their baby son, Gareth, aged five months, our first grand-child. As you would expect, coming from such a lineage, he is an exquisite child, who behaves perfectly and never puts a foot wrong! Consequently I am a bit at a loss to explain why he was wakeful and noisy that night to such an extent that his distracted mother got little or no sleep at all and was more than willing to sell him to the highest bidder the following morning. Fortunately, an angel of mercy, in the form of her sister, Rachel, appeared and saved her sanity by whisking him away immediately and taking charge, leaving the harassed bride-to-be to a short but well-earned rest. Rachel brought the baby into my bedroom so that I could have a cuddle while she prepared his breakfast. It was love-ly to have him all to myself for ten minutes, without having to feel guilty about not getting up.

At 10.30 am, Jenny drove the four girls (including me) to the hair-dresser's. While we were there, the three others had their head-dresses put on as well. As we drove home again, other drivers were looking askance at this girl, driving somewhat erratically, and wearing a wreath of flowers on her head, which seemed strangely at odds with her jeans and T-shirt. A couple of minutes after we got home, the flowers were delivered. They were cream-coloured orchids and pale yellow roses, and they set off Jenny's ivory dress and Nancy's and Rachel's sea-green taffeta to perfection.

I had spent eight weeks in Walton Neurology Centre a year ago, to have my medication reviewed and revised and since then my mobility in the mornings has greatly improved, so I wasn't surprised that I had been coping well so far. However, knowing from experience that 3.00 pm onwards was always hazardous, I was expecting problems later.

By 2.45 pm we were all ready. The girls looked so lovely that I felt a lump rise up in my throat and had to fight back the tears. I've always found it a little incongruous that we should cry when we are happy! The three men wore grey lounge-suits and cravats to match the Bridesmaids dresses. The two ushers, Gregory and Paul's youngest brother, Geoffrey, wore white shirts, black striped trousers and bow-ties and cummerbunds in the same colour as the Bridesmaids. I was amazed that I had been steady enough to put on my own make-up, change into my suit, with navy accessories, without encountering any difficulty. Now here I was having photos taken, looking as poised and relaxed as the rest of them. I had worried about having to walk down the Church aisle, because I knew I would be feeling very nervous, and in such circumstances I usually give a very convincing performance as a stringed puppet! However, anyone who may have been expecting a free cabaret on this particular occasion was doomed to disappointment. In actual fact, much to everyone's total surprise (not to mention my own), I negotiated it as effortlessly as the rest of the guests, although I was glad to have Adrian, Nancy's boyfriend, to walk with me just in case I should disintegrate, but

I did not. *Not* during the Church service, *Not* afterwards in the church grounds, where the professional photos were taken, *Not* at the Reception Buffet, *Not* even at the Evening Disco, where I danced the night away! Our family, friends and relatives were astonished and wondered if perhaps I had been given an additional dose of something, over and above my normal medication. I assured them I had not and that I was as mystified as they were. To be able to look and feel so normal without making any effort was like being in someone else's body! I found the experience wonderfully exhilarating, but I was wondering all the time, what was making it happen, especially when I had expected a totally opposite reaction. There must be an explanation! If only we could fathom it, it might help to uncover the root cause and thereby come closer to finding a possible cure for this very distressing and highly debilitating condition.

❁

❀

Calling All Parkinsonians!

The Rhythm Method
Re-Examined

❀

❀

Those of you who, having read the title of this article, are preparing to turn the page, concluding, somewhat prematurely, that it is not for you, please:

STOP. WAIT. THINK AGAIN!

Read on and you will soon discover that it is not, as you thought, an in-depth study of an age-old method of contraception (which was not particularly efficient anyway) No, it is something far more fascinating and liberating. It is an up-to-date, revolutionary process by which you can regain dignity and, with it, essential mobility when you find yourself glued to the middle of the road in a crowded thoroughfare on Market day. When you risk being trampled to death, if not indeed run over, by hooting vehicles and busy shoppers – who are thinking, not of you, but of their next purchase – dragging their gaping, unwilling offspring along backwards behind them! Sounds only too familiar? Me too – until I gradually discovered that PD responds to a rhythm.

This phenomenon only dawned on me a few months ago (I've had PD for almost thirteen years now, but I'm a slow learner). I have always enjoyed listening and dancing to 'POP' music, particularly '60s and '70s and the radio is on most of the day – tuned in to the radio stations which play this kind of music. I became aware that I was automatically walking in time to the beat of whichever record happened to be playing. After I had noticed it the first few times, I decided to see if it would work when I was 'off' – it did! I was elated and kept trying it to different songs with varied rhythms, with similar results. Although there were times when it did not work, these were times when my immobility was chronic, and at those times nothing works!

Not long afterwards, I experimented using regular patterns on carpets as 'stepping stones'. My success fascinated me. However, this did not help me at home, because all our carpets are plain. I was stumped, until I hit upon the idea of using the stains as my 'stepping stones'! Then the inevitable day dawned when we had to have the carpets cleaned – foiled again! That stopped me in my tracks. But not for long. I am now campaigning to get the stains back!

Before I finish, I have one more alternative to suggest. This one was suggested to me by my daughter, Nancy, whom some of you may have met at the first 'International Yapmeet' in Peterborough earlier this year. Her idea was to try walking in step with someone. (If there's no one with you, grab the first person you see and threaten to turn into a pumpkin if they are disinclined to help.) I have been agreeably surprised at how effective the 'in step' method has proved itself to be. However, it only works on straight lines, not on corners, so if I drop off the end of the world, you'll know why! AAAAAAAAAAAAAAAAH – I spoke too soon!

❀

❀

LOVE IS....
THE ESSENCE OF LIFE

'I can fly higher than an eagle
And you are the wind beneath my wings.'

Yes, you are my strength, my fortitude,
In you I put my trust
You are the one to whom I cling
When icy winds prevail

Those ice-cold blasts of selfishness
of hate and disillusion,
Those moods of black despair and fear
That converge and prey upon my mind
When Darkness fills my day.

You are the one who's always there,
Who cares enough to find me
And instil in me the courage
I need to face the truth

The enemy is already close
And moving ever nearer,
Treading heavily, as he does
Upon the circumference of my life
Intruding on my personal space
Threatening to seize it,
Leaving nothing but a void.

A deep and yawning chasm
Filled only with my failures
Into which I shall surely fall
And perish in iniquity

But before I do
You will come to my aid,
You will feel my fear
And be with me

You will buoy me up
On the crest of your smile
Your faith in me
Will keep me afloat

I'll soar way up to the heavens
And sail in a clear blue sky,
As long as you are with me
there's nothing I cannot do

Yes! 'I can fly higher than an eagle
And you are the wind beneath my wings.'

❀

Current Medication

8.00	1 Bromocriptine	5mg
	1 Bromocriptine	2.5mg
	1 Madopar	62.5
	1 Benzhexol	2mg
11.30	2 Bromocriptine	5mg
13.00	1 Bromocriptine	5mg
	1 Bromocriptine	2.5mg
	1 Madopar	62.5
16.30	1 Bromocriptine	5mg
18.00	1 Bromocriptine	5mg
	1 Bromocriptine	2.5mg
	1 Madopar	62.5
22.00	1 Madopar	62.5
	1 Amitriptyline	50mg

I have recently acquired a 'Dreaded Contraption' (wheel chair), which spends the majority of its life banished within a dark closet, from which it is liberated only at times of dire necessity, as a last resort, when all other alternatives have been exhausted (including the person who drew the short straw and is consequently obliged to operate it).

❀

Epilogue

❀

Epilogue

When we first found out that mum had Parkinson's, we didn't know what this would mean except that she wouldn't die from it, and because she was young it wouldn't progress quickly. Both Mum and Dad tried not to let it affect our lives as a family. Ignoring it, Mum entered into all normal activities, just at a slower pace, never openly complaining about it, which meant life carried on largely unchanged for at least eight years. At the same time we knew Mum had her outlet through poetry – and later this book – discovering the computer, a major influence on her life.

Gradually Mum and all of us have grown to live with it more. Mum uses her sense of humour to put people at their ease with it, and recently did a voice background on an amateur video about it. However it is constantly difficult to accept. Mum is naturally reserved and is very self concious about what people think about her condition, even though they probably don't think that much at all. Then there are the daily struggles which we hate to see her having to battle through – it seems so unfair – the unpredictability and the cruelty with which it sometimes affects what seems like everything : reading, sleeping, voice, energy, back and movement. We feel sad and frustrated at the limitations on her life, restricting what she can do with Dad, us and her grandchildren, which is particularly hard as she loves children so much.

Sometimes the unpredictability can be encouraging, because there is no definite course and people with Parkinson's exhibit very different symptoms. There is also the hope of improved medicines. Most importantly, it is a condition where we still have her, her full personality with us. She has always been there for us as a mother – Parkinson's can't take that away, or the fact that we need her very much.

In this book Mum has managed to condense all her frustrations and has shown how her sense of humour and inner strength help her to still enjoy life. We hope that other families in a similar situation will find comfort from reading it.

Nancy, Jenny, Rachel and Gregory.

❀